THE WAY OF THE SHIP: SAILORS, SHANTIES AND SHANTYMEN

THE WAY OF THE SHIP: SAILORS, SHANTIES AND SHANTYMEN

BY

RICHARD RUNCIMAN TERRY,

FOREWORD BY SIR WALTER RUNCIMAN

Fireship Press
www.FireshipPress.com

The Way of the Ship: Sailors: Shanties and Shantymen
Copyright © 2008 by Fireship Press

ISBN-13: 978-1-934757-61-1
ISBN-10: 1-934757-61-6

BISAC Subject Headings:
    MUS017000 MUSIC / Genres & Styles / Folk & Traditional
    HIS027150   HISTORY / Military / Naval

This work is based on the following:

Terry, Richard Runciman. *The Shanty Book Part I Sailor Shanties* London: J. Curwen & Sons Ltd., 1921

Terry, Richard Runciman. *The Shanty Book Part II Sailor Shanties* London: J. Curwen & Sons Ltd., 1926

Address all correspondence to:
Fireship Press, LLC
P.O. Box 68412
Tucson, AZ 85737

Or visit our website at:
www.FireshipPress.com

THE WAY OF THE SHIP
PART I

SHANTY SONGS - PART I

THE WAY OF THE SHIP
PART II

ALPHABETICAL INDEX OF SHANTIES

THE WAY OF THE SHIP
PART I

FOREWORD
BY SIR WALTER RUNCIMAN

It is sometimes difficult for old sailors like myself to realize that these fine shanty tunes—so fascinating to the musician, and which no sailor can hear without emotion—died out with the sailing vessel, and now belong to a chapter of maritime history that is definitely closed. They will never more be heard on the face of the waters, but it is well that they should be preserved with reverent care, as befits a legacy from the generation of seamen that came to an end with the stately vessels they manned with such skill and resource.

In speech, the old-time 'shellback' was notoriously reticent—almost inarticulate; but in song he found self-expression, and all the romance and poetry of the sea are breathed into his shanties, where simple childlike sentimentality alternates with the Rabelaisian humour of the grown man. Whatever landsmen may think about shanty words—with their cheerful inconsequence, or light-hearted coarseness—there can be no two opinions about the tunes, which, as folk-music, are a national asset.

I know, of course, that several shanty collections are in the market, but as a sailor I am bound to say that only one—Capt. W.B. Whall's 'Sea Songs, Ships, and Shanties'—can be regarded as authoritative. Only a portion of Capt. Whall's delightful book is devoted to shanties, of which he prints the melodies only (without accompaniment); and of these he does not profess to give more than those he himself learnt at sea. I am glad, therefore, to welcome Messrs. Curwen's project of a wide and representative collection. Dr. Terry's qualifications as editor are exceptional, since he was reared in an environment of nineteenth-century seamen, and is the only landsman I have met who is able to render shanties as the old seamen did. I am not musician enough to criticize his pianoforte accompaniments, but I can vouch for the authenticity of the *melodies* as he presents them, untampered with in any way.

WALTER RUNCIMAN
Shoreston Hall,
Chathill, 1921

AN INTRODUCTION TO
THE SHANTY

APOLOGIA

It may reasonably be asked by what authority a mere landsman publishes a book on a nautical subject. I may, therefore, plead in extenuation that I have all my life been closely connected with seafaring matters, especially during childhood and youth, and have literally 'grown up with' shanties. My maternal ancestors followed the sea as far back as the family history can be traced, and sailor uncles and grand-uncles have sung shanties to me from my childhood upwards. During boyhood I was constantly about amongst ships, and had learnt at first hand all the popular shanties before any collection of them appeared in print. I have in later years collected them from all manner of sailors, chiefly at Northumbrian sources. I have collated these later versions with those which I learnt at first hand as a boy from sailor relatives, and also aboard ship. And lastly, I lived for some years in the West Indies, one of the few remaining spots where shanties may still be heard, where my chief recreation was cruising round the islands in my little ketch. In addition to hearing them in West Indian seaports, aboard Yankee sailing ships and sugar droghers, I also heard them sung constantly on shore in Antigua under rather curious conditions.

West Indian negro shanties are movable wooden huts, and when a family wishes to change its *venue* it does so in the following manner: The shanty is levered up on to a low platform on wheels, to which two very long ropes are attached. The ropes are manned by as many hands as their length will admit. A 'shantyman' mounts the roof of the hut and sits astride it. He sings a song which has a chorus, and is an exact musical parallel of a seaman's 'pull-and-haul' shanty. The crowd below sings the chorus, giving a pull on the rope at the required points in the music, just as sailors did when hauling at sea. Each pull on the rope draws the hut a short distance forward, and the process is continued till its final resting-place is reached, when the shantyman descends from the roof. The hut is then levered off the platform on to *terra firma* and fixed in its required position.

WHAT A SHANTY IS

Shanties were labor songs sung by sailors of the merchant service only while at work, and never by way of recreation. Moreover—at least, in the nineteenth century—they were never used aboard men-o'-war, where all orders were carried out in silence to the pipe of the bo'sun's whistle.

Before the days of factories and machinery, all forms of work were literally *manual* labor, and all the world over the laborer, obeying a primitive instinct, sang at his toil: the harvester with his sickle, the weaver at the loom, the spinner at the wheel. Long after machinery had driven the labor-song from the land it survived at sea in the form of shanties, since all work aboard a sailing vessel was performed by hand.

The advent of screw steamers sounded the death-knell of the shanty. Aboard the steamer there were practically no sails to be manipulated; the donkey-engine and steam winch supplanted the hand-worked windlass and capstan. By the end of the seventies steam had driven the sailing ship from the seas. A number of sailing vessels lingered on through the eighties, but they retained little of the corporate pride and splendour that was once theirs. The old spirit was gone never to return.

When the sailing ship ruled the waters and the shanty was a living thing no one appears to have paid heed to it. To the landsman of those days—before folk-song hunting had begun —the haunting beauty of the tunes would appear to have made no appeal. This may be partly accounted for by the fact that he would never be likely to hear the sailor sing them ashore, and partly because of the Rabelaisian character of the words to which they were sung aboard ship. We had very prim notions of propriety in those days, and were apt to overlook the beauty of the melodies, and to speak of shanties in bulk as 'low vulgar songs.' Be that as it may, it was not until the late eighties—when the shanty was beginning to die out with the sailing ship—that any attempt was made to form a collection.

ORIGIN OF THE WORD

Here let me enter my protest against the literary preciosity which derives the word from (*un*) *chante* and spells it 'chanty'—in other words, against the gratuitous assumption that unlettered British sailors derived one of the commonest words in their vocabulary from a foreign source. The result of this 'literary' spelling is that ninety-nine landsmen out of every hundred, instead of pronouncing the word 'shanty,' rhyming with 'scanty' (*as every sailor did*), pronounce it 'tchahnty,' rhyming with 'auntie,' thereby courting the amusement or contempt of every seaman. The vogue of '*c*hanty' was apparently created by the late W.E. Henley, a fine poet, a great man of letters, a profound admirer of shanty tunes, but entirely unacquainted with nautical affairs. Kipling and other landsmen have given additional currency to the spelling. The 'literary' sailors, Clark Russell and Frank Bullen, have also spelt it '*c*hanty,' but their reason is obvious. The modest seaman always bowed before the landsman's presumed superiority in 'book-larnin.' What more natural than that Russell and Bullen, obsessed by so ancient a tradition, should accept uncritically the landsman's spelling. But educated sailors devoid of 'literary' pretensions have always written the word as it was pronounced. To my mind the strongest argument against the literary landsman's derivation of the word is that the British sailor cultivated the supremest contempt for everything French, and would be the last person to label such a definitely British practice as shanty-singing with a French title. If there had been such a thing in French ships as a labor-song bearing such a far-fetched title as (*un*) *chante*, there might have been a remote possibility of the British sailor adopting the French term in a spirit of sport or derision, but there is no evidence that any such practice, or any such term, achieved any vogue in French ships. As a matter of fact, the Oxford Dictionary (which prints it '*s*hanty') states that the word never found its way into print until 1869.

The truth is that, however plausible the French derivation theory may sound, it is after all pure speculation—and a landsman's speculation at that—unsupported by a shred of concrete evidence.

If I wished to advance another theory more plausible still, and equally unconvincing, I might urge that the word was derived from the negro hut-removals already mentioned. Here, at least, we have a very ancient custom, which would be familiar to British seamen visiting West Indian seaports. The object moved was a *shanty*; the music accompanying the operation was called, by the negroes, a *shanty* tune; its musical form (solo and chorus) was identical with the sailor *shanty*; the pulls on the rope followed the same method which obtained at sea; the soloist was called a *shanty*man; like the shantyman at sea he did no work, but merely extemporized verses to which the workers at the ropes supplied the chorus; and finally, the negroes still pronounce the word itself exactly as the seaman did.

I am quite aware of the flaws in the above argument, but at least it shows a manual labor act performed both afloat and ashore under precisely similar conditions as to (a) its nature, (b) its musical setting; called by the same name, *with the same pronunciation* in each case; and lastly, connected, in one case, with an actual hut or *shanty*. Against this concrete argument we have a landsman's abstract speculation, which (a) begs the whole question, and (b) which was never heard of until a few years before the disappearance of the sailing ship. I do not assert that the negroid derivation is conclusive, but that from (*un*) *chante* will not bear serious inspection.

BIBLIOGRAPHY

The material under this head is very scanty. Nothing of any consequence was written before the eighties, when W.L. Alden, in *Harper's Magazine*, and James Runciman, in the *St. James' Gazette* and other papers, wrote articles on the subject with musical quotations. Since then several collections have appeared:

1887. *Sailors' Songs or Chanties*, the words by Frederick J. Davis, R.N.R., the music composed and arranged upon traditional sailor airs by Ferris Tozer, Mus. D. Oxon.

1888. *The Music of the Waters*, by Laura Alexandrine Smith.

1910 and 1912. *Sea Songs, Ships, and Shanties*, by Capt. W.B. Whall.

1912. *Songs of Sea Labor*, by Frank T. Bullen and W.F. Arnold.

1914. *English Folk Chanteys* with Pianoforte Accompaniment, collected by Cecil J. Sharp.

Of all these collections Capt. Whall's is the only one which a sailor could accept as authoritative. Capt. Whall unfortunately only gives the twenty-eight shanties which he himself learnt at sea. But to any one who has heard them sung aboard the old sailing ships, his versions ring true, and have a bite and a snap that is lacking in those published by mere collectors.

Davis and Tozer's book has had a great vogue, as it was for many years the only one on the market. But the statement that the music is 'composed and arranged on traditional sailor airs' rules it out of court in the eyes of seamen, since (a) a sailor song is not a shanty, and (b) to 'compose and arrange on traditional airs' is to destroy the traditional form.

Miss Smith's book is a thick volume into which was tumbled indiscriminately and uncritically a collection of all sorts of tunes from all sorts of countries which had any connection with seas, lakes, rivers, or their geographical equivalents. Scientific folk-song collecting was not understood in those days, and consequently all was fish that came to the authoress' net. Sailor shanties and landsmen's nautical effusions were jumbled together higgledy-piggledy, along with 'Full Fathom Five' and the 'Eton Boating Song.' But this lack of discrimination, pardonable in those days, was not so serious as the inability to write the tunes down correctly. So long as they were copied from other song-books they were not so bad, but when it came to taking them down from the seamen's singing the results were deplorable. Had the authoress been able to give us correct versions of the shanties her collection would have been a valuable one. The book contains altogether about thirty-two shanties collected from sailors in the Tyne seaports. Since both Miss Smith and myself hail from Newcastle, her 'hunting ground' for shanties was also mine, and I am consequently in a position to assess the importance or unimportance of her work. I may, therefore, say that although hardly a single shanty is noted down correctly, I can see clearly—having myself noted the same tunes in the same district—what she intended to convey, and furthermore can vouch for the accuracy of some of the words which were common to north country sailors, and which have not appeared in other collections.

If I have been obliged to criticize Miss Smith's book it is not because I wish to disparage a well-intentioned effort, but because I constantly hear *The Music of the Waters* quoted as an authoritative work on sailor shanties; and since the shanties in it were all collected in the district where I spent boyhood and youth, I am familiar with all of them, and can state definitely that they are in no sense authoritative. I should like, however, to pay my tribute of respect to Miss Smith's industry, and to her enterprise in calling attention to tunes that then seemed in a fair way to disappear.

Bullen and Arnold's book ought to have been a valuable contribution to shanty literature, as Bullen certainly knew his shanties, and used to sing them capitally. Unfortunately his musical collaborator does not appear to have been gifted with the faculty of taking down authentic versions from his singing. He seems to have had difficulty in differentiating between long measured notes and unmeasured pauses; between the respective meanings of three-four and six-eight time; between modal and modern tunes; and between the cases where irregular barring was or was not required. Apart from the amateur nature of the harmonies, the book exhibits such strange unacquaintance with the rudiments of musical notation as the following (p. 25):

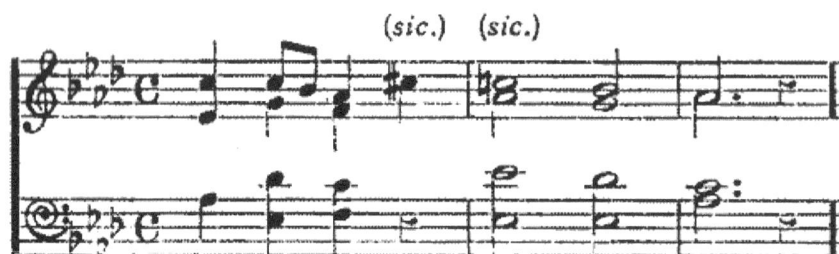

A few other collections deserve mention:

1912. *The Esperance Morris Book*, Part II (Curwen Edition 8571), contains five shanties collected and arranged by Clive Carey.

1914. *Shanties and Forebitters*, collected and accompaniments written by Mrs. Clifford Beckett (Curwen Edition 6293).

Journal of the Folk-Song Society, Nos. 12, 18, and 20, contain articles on shanties, with musical examples (melodies only), which, from the academic point of view, are not without interest.

1920. *The Motherland Song Book* (Vols. III and IV, edited by R. Vaughan Williams) contains seven shanties. It is worthy of note that Dr. Vaughan Williams, Mr. Clive Carey, and Mrs. Clifford Beckett all spell the word 'shanty' as sailors pronounced it.

1920. *Sailor Shanties arranged for Solo and Chorus of Men's Voices* by the present editor; two selections (Curwen Edition 50571 and 50572).

There are one or two other collections in print which are obviously compilations, showing no original research. Of these I make no note.

SHANTY FORMS

Shanties may be roughly divided, as regards their use, into two classes: (a) Hauling shanties, and (b) Windlass and Capstan. The former class accompanied the setting of the sails, and the latter the weighing of the anchor, or 'warping her in' to the wharf, etc. Capstan shanties were also used for pumping ship. A few shanties were 'interchangeable,' i.e. they were used for both halliards and capstan. The subdivisions of each class are interesting, and the nature of the work involving 'walk away,' 'stamp and go,' 'sweating her up,' 'hand over hand,' and other types of shanty would make good reading; but nautical details, however fascinating, must be economized in a musical publication.

Capstan shanties are readily distinguishable by their music. The operation of walking round the capstan (pushing the capstan bars in front of them) was continuous and not intermittent. Both tune and chorus were, as a rule, longer than those of the hauling shanty, and there was much greater variety of rhythm. Popular songs, if they had a chorus or refrain, could be, and were, effectively employed for windlass and capstan work.

Hauling shanties were usually shorter than capstan ones, and are of two types: (a) those used for 'the long hoist' and (b) those required for 'the short pull' or 'sweating-up.'

Americans called these operations the 'long' and the 'short drag.' The former was used when beginning to hoist sails, when the gear would naturally be slack and moderately easy to manipulate. It had two short choruses, with a double pull in each. In the following example, the pulls are marked with a "^" sign.

REUBEN RANZO

It is easy to see how effective a collective pull at each of these points would be, while the short intervals of solo would give time for shifting the hands on the rope and making ready for the next combined effort.

When the sail was fully hoisted and the gear taut, a much stronger pull was necessary in order to make everything fast, so the shanty was then changed for a 'sweating-up' one, in which there was only one short chorus and one very strong pull:

HAUL THE BOWLIN'

So much effort was now required on the pull that it was difficult to sing a musical note at that point. The last word was therefore usually shouted.

SOURCES OF TUNES

The sailor travelled in many lands, and in his shanties there are distinct traces of the nationalities of the countries he visited. Without doubt a number of them came from American negro sources. The songs heard on Venetian gondolas must have had their effect, as many examples show. There are also distinct traces of folk-songs which the sailor would have learnt ashore in his native fishing village, and the more familiar Christy Minstrel song was frequently pressed into the service. As an old sailor once said to me: 'You can make anything into a shanty.'

Like all traditional tunes, some shanties are in the ancient modes, and others in the modern major and minor keys. It is the habit of the 'folk-songer' (I am not alluding to our recognized folk-song experts) to find 'modes' in every traditional tune. It will suffice, therefore, to say that shanties follow the course of all other traditional music. Many are modern, and easily recognizable as such. Others are modal in character, such as 'What shall we do with the drunken sailor?' No. 14, and 'The Hog's-Eye Man,' No. 11. Others fulfil to a certain extent modal conditions, but are nevertheless in keys, e.g. 'Stormalong John,' No. 10.

Like many other folk-songs, certain shanties—originally, no doubt, in a mode—were, by the insertion of leading notes, converted into the minor key. There was also the tendency on the part of the modern sailor to turn his minor key into a major one. I sometimes find sailors singing in the major, nowadays, tunes which the very old men of my boyhood used to sing in the minor. A case in point is 'Haul away, Joe.' Miss Smith is correct in giving it in the minor form which once obtained on the Tyne, and I am inclined to hazard the opinion that that was the original form and not, as now, the following:

Way, haul a - way, We'll haul a-way the bow - lin'.

Way, haul a - way, We'll haul a - way, Joe.

In later times I have also heard 'The Drunken Sailor' (a distinctly modal tune) sung in the major as follows:

What shall we do with the drunken sai - lor?

What shall we do with the drunken sai - lor?

I have generally found that these perversions of the tunes are due to sailors who took to the sea as young men in the last days of the sailing ship, and consequently did not imbibe to the full the old traditions. With the intolerance of youth they assumed that the modal turn given to a shanty by the older sailor was the mark of ignorance, since it did not square with their ideas of a major or minor key. This experience is common to all folk-tune collectors.

Other characteristics, for example: (a) different words to the same melody; (b) different melodies to the same or similar words, need not be enlarged upon here, as they will be self-evident when a definitive collection is published.

Of the usual troubles incidental to folk-song collecting it is unnecessary to speak. But the collection of shanties involves difficulties of a special kind. In taking down a folk-song from a rustic, one's chief difficulty is surmounted when one has broken down his shyness and induced him to sing. There is nothing for him to do then but get on with the song. Shanties, however, being labor songs, one is 'up against' the strong psychological connection between the song and its manual acts. Two illustrations will explain what I mean.

A friend of mine who lives in Kerry wished a collector to hear some of the traditional keening, and an old woman with the reputation of being the best keener in the district, when brought to the house to sing the funeral chants, made several attempts and then replied in a distressed manner: 'I can't do it; there's no body,' This did not mean that she was unwilling to keen in the absence of a corpse, but that she was unable to do so. Just before giving up in despair my friend was seized with a brain wave, and asked her if it would suffice for him to lie down on the floor and personate the corpse. When he had done this the old woman found herself able to get on with the keening.

An incident related to me quite casually by Sir Walter Runciman throws a similar light on the inseparability of a shanty and its labor. He described how one evening several north country ships happened to be lying in a certain port. All the officers and crews were ashore, leaving only the apprentices aboard, some of whom, as he remarked, were 'very keen on shanties,' and their suggestion of passing away the time by singing some was received with enthusiasm. The whole party of about thirty apprentices at once collected themselves aboard one vessel, sheeted home the main topsail, and commenced to haul it up to the tune of 'Boney was a warrior,' changing to 'Haul the Bowlin'' for 'sweating-up.' In the enthusiasm of their singing, and the absence of any officer to call "Vast hauling,' they continued operations until they broke the topsail yard in two, when the sight of the wreckage and the fear of consequences brought the singing to an abrupt conclusion. In my then ignorance I naturally asked: 'Why couldn't you have sung shanties without hoisting the topsail?' and the reply was: 'How could we sing a shanty without having our hands on the rope?' Here we have the whole psychology of the labor-song: the old woman could not keen without the 'body,' and the young apprentices could not sing shanties apart from the work to which they belonged. The only truly satisfactory results which I ever get nowadays from an old sailor are when he has been stimulated by conversation to become reminiscent, and croons his shanties almost subconsciously. Whenever I find a sailor willing to declaim shanties in the style of a song I begin to be a little suspicious of his seamanship. In one of the journals of the Folk-Song Society there is an account of a sailor who formed a little party of seafaring men to give public performances of shanties on the concert platform. No doubt this was an interesting experience for the listeners, but that a self-conscious performance such as this could represent the old shanty singing I find it difficult to believe. Of course I have had sailors sing shanties to me in a fine declamatory manner, but I usually found one of three things to be the case: the man was a 'sea lawyer,' or had not done much deep-sea sailing; or his seamanship only dated from the decline of the sailing vessel.

It is doubtless interesting to the folk-singer to see in print shanties taken down from an individual sailor with his individual melodic twirls and twiddles. But since no two sailors ever sing the same shanty quite in the same manner, there must necessarily be some means of getting at the tune, unhampered by these individual idiosyncrasies, which are quite a different thing from what folk-song students recognize as 'variants.' The power to discriminate can only be acquired by familiarity with the shanty as it was in its palmy days. The collector who comes upon the scene at this late time of day must necessarily be at a disadvantage. The ordinary methods which he would apply to a folk-song break down in the case of a labor-song. Manual actions were the soul of the shanty; eliminate these and you have only the skeleton of what was once a living thing. It is quite possible, I know, to push this line of argument too far, but every one who knows anything about seamanship must feel that a shanty nowadays cannot be other than a pale reflection of what it once was.

That is why I deprecate the spurious authenticity conferred by print upon isolated versions of shanties sung by individual old men. When the originals are available it seems to me pedantic and academic to put into print the comic mispronunciations of well-known words by old and uneducated seamen.

And this brings me to the last difficulty which confronts the collector with no previous knowledge of shanties. As a mere matter of dates, any sailors now remaining from sailing ship days must necessarily be very old men. I have found that their octogenarian memories are not always to be trusted. On one occasion an old man sang quite glibly a tune which was in reality a *pasticcio* of three separate shanties all known to me. I have seen similar results in print, since the collector arrived too late upon the scene to be able to detect the tricks which an old man's memory played him.

One final remark about collectors which has an important bearing upon the value of their work. There were two classes of sailing vessels that sailed from English ports—the coaster or the mere collier that plied between the Tyne or Severn and Boulogne, and the Southspainer, under which term was comprised all deep-sea vessels. On the collier or short-voyage vessel the crew was necessarily a small one, and the shanty was more or less of a makeshift, adapted to the capacity of the limited numbers of the crew. Purely commercial reasons precluded the engagement of any shantyman specially distinguished for his musical attainments. Consequently, so far as the shanty was concerned, 'any old thing would do.' On the Southspainer, however, things were very different. The shantyman was usually a person of considerable musical importance, who sang his songs in a more or less finished manner; his melodies were clean, clear-cut things, without any of the folk-songer's quavers and wobbles. I heard them in the 'seventies and 'eighties before the sailing-ship had vanished, consequently I give them as they were then sung—undisfigured and unobscured by the mixture of twirls, quavers, and hiccups one hears from octogenarian mariners who attempt them to-day.

METHOD OF SINGING

So far as the music was concerned, a shanty was a song with a chorus. The song was rendered by one singer, called the shantyman, and the chorus by the sailors who performed their work in time with the music. So far as the words were concerned there was usually a stereotyped opening of one or more verses. For all succeeding verses the shantyman improvized words, and his topics were many and varied, the most appreciated naturally being personal allusions to the crew and officers, sarcastic criticism on the quality of the food, wistful references to the good time coming on shore, etc. There was no need for any connection or relevancy between one verse or another, nor were rhymes required. The main thing that mattered was that the rhythm should be preserved and that the words should be such as would keep the workers merry or interested. Once the stereotyped verses were got rid of and the improvisation began, things became so intimate and personal as to be unprintable. It was a curious fact that such shanty words as lent themselves most to impropriety were wedded to tunes either of fine virility or haunting sweetness.

For 'pull-and-haul' shanties the shantyman took up his position near the workers and announced the shanty, sometimes by singing the first line. This established the tune to which they were to supply the chorus. For capstan shanties he usually did the same. He frequently sat on the capstan, but so far as I can learn he more usually took up his position on or against the knightheads. The importance of the shantyman could not be overestimated. A good shantyman with a pretty wit was worth his weight in gold. He was a privileged person, and was excused all work save light or odd jobs.

THE WORDS OF SHANTIES

I have already noted the shanties which were derived from popular songs, also the type which contained a definite narrative. Except where a popular song was adapted, the form was usually rhymed or more often unrhymed couplets. The topics were many and varied, but the chief ones were: (1) popular heroes such as Napoleon, and 'Santy Anna.' That the British sailor of the eighteenth century should hate every Frenchman and yet make a hero of Bonaparte is one of the mysteries which has never been explained. Another mystery is the fascination which Antonio Lopez de Santa Anna (1795-1876) exercised over the sailor. He was one of the many Mexican 'Presidents' and was defeated by the American General Taylor in 1847. That did not prevent the British sailor presenting him in the light of an invariable victor until he was led out to be shot (he really died a natural death) by persons unknown. (2) The sailor had mythical heroes too, e.g. 'Ranzo,' already mentioned, and 'Stormy,' who was the theme of many shanties. No sailor could ever give the least explanation of them, and so they remain the last echoes of long forgotten sagas. (3) High-sounding, poetic, or mysterious words, such as 'Lowlands,' 'Shenandoah,' 'Rolling river,' 'Hilo,' 'Mobile Bay,' 'Rio Grande,' had a great fascination, as their constant recurrence in many shanties shows. (4) The sailor also sang much of famous ships, such as 'The Flying Cloud,' 'The Henry Clay,' or 'The Victory,' and famous lines, such as 'The Black Ball.' Even famous shipowners were celebrated in song, as witness 'Mr. John Tapscott,' in 'We're all bound to go.' (5) Love affairs, in which 'Lizer Lee' and other damsels constantly figured, were an endless topic. (6) But chiefly did Jack sing of affairs connected with his ship. He never sang of 'the rolling main,' 'the foaming billows,' 'the storm clouds,' etc. These are the stock-in-trade of the landsman; they were too real for the sailor to sing about. He had the instinct of the primitive man which forbids mention of natural forces of evil omen. But intimate or humorous matters such as the failings of his officers, the quality of the food, the rate of pay, or other grievances were treated with vigor and emphasis. Like the Britisher of to-day, he would put up with any hardship so long as he were permitted to grouse about it. The shantyman gave humorous expression to this grousing, which deprived it of the element of sulks. Steam let off in this way was a wholesome preventive of mutiny.

The choruses were usually jingles, with no relevance save maintenance of the rhythm.

One feature of the words may be noted. The sailor's instinct for romance was so strong that in his choruses, at least, no matter how 'hair-curling' the solo might be, he always took the crude edge off the concrete and presented it as an abstraction if possible. For example, he knew perfectly well that one meaning of 'to blow' was to knock or kick. He knew that discipline in Yankee packets was maintained by corporeal methods, so much so that the Mates, to whom the function of knocking the 'packet rats' about was delegated, were termed first, second, and third 'blowers,' or strikers, and in the shanty he sang 'Blow the man down.' 'Knock' or 'kick,' as I have recently seen in a printed collection, was too crudely realistic for him. In like manner the humorous title, 'Hog's-eye,' veiled the coarse intimacy of the term which it represented. And that is where, when collecting shanties from the 'longshore' mariner of to-day, I find him, if he is uneducated, so tiresome. He not only wants to explain to me as a landsman the exact meaning (which I know already) of terms which the old type of sailor, with his natural delicacy, avoided discussing, but he tries where possible to work them into his shanty, a thing the sailor of old time never did. So that when one sees in print expressions which sailors did not use, it is presumptive evidence that the collector has been imposed upon by a salt of the 'sea lawyer' type.

Perhaps I ought to make this point clearer. Folk-song collecting was once an artistic pursuit. Now it has become a flourishing industry of high commercial value. From the commercial point of view it is essential that results should be printed and circulated as widely as possible. Some knowledge of seamanship is an absolute necessity where folk-shanties are concerned. The mere collector nowadays does not possess that knowledge; it is confined to those who have had practical experience of the sea, but who will never print their experiences. The mere collector *must* print his versions. What is unprinted must remain unknown; what is printed is therefore accepted as authoritative, however misleading it may be. Many highly educated men, of whom Captain Whall is the type, have followed the sea. It is from them that the only really trustworthy information is forthcoming. But so far as I can judge, it is uneducated men who appear to sing to collectors nowadays, and I have seen many a quiet smile on the lips of the educated sailor when he is confronted with printed versions of the uneducated seaman's performances. For example, one of the best known of all shanties is 'The Hog's-eye man'; I have seen this entitled 'The Hog-eyed man,' and even 'The Ox-eyed man.' Every old sailor knew the meaning of the term. Whall and Bullen, who were both sailors, use the correct expression, 'Hog-eye.' The majority of sailors of my acquaintance called it 'Hog's-eye.' Did decency permit I could show conclusively how Whall and Bullen are right and the mere collector wrong. It must suffice, however, for me to say that the term 'Hog's-eye' or 'Hog-eye' had nothing whatever to do with the optic of the 'man' who was sung about. I could multiply instances, but this one is typical and must suffice.

We hear a great deal of the coarseness and even lewdness of the shanty, but I could wish a little more stress were laid on the sailor's natural delicacy. Jack was always a gentleman in feeling. Granted his drinking, cursing, and amours—but were not these, until Victorian times, the hall-mark of every gentleman ashore? The Rabelaisian jokes of the shantyman were solos, the sound of which would not travel far beyond the little knot of workers who chuckled over them. The choruses—shouted out by the whole working party—would be heard all over the ship and even penetrate ashore if she were in port. Hence, in not a single instance do the choruses of any shanty contain a coarse expression.

EDITORIAL METHODS

As regards the tunes, I have adhered to the principle of giving each one as it was sung by some individual singer. This method has not been applied to the words. Consequently the verses of any given shanty may have derived from any number of singers. Since there was no connection or relevancy between the different verses of a shanty, the only principle I have adhered to is that whatever verses are set down should have been sung to me at some time or other by some sailor or other.

Of course I have had to camouflage many unprintable expressions, and old sailors will readily recognize where this has been done. Sometimes a whole verse (after the first line) has needed camouflage, and the method adopted is best expressed as follows:

> There was a young lady of Gloucester
> Who couldn't eat salt with her egg,
> And when she sat down
> She could never get up,
> And so the poor dog had none.

As regards the accompaniments, I have been solely guided by the necessity of preserving the character of the melodies in all their vigor and vitality, and have tried, even in obviously modal tunes, not to obscure their breeziness by academic treatment.

ACKNOWLEDGMENTS

Amongst those to whom I owe thanks, I must number the Editors of *The Music Student* and *Music and Letters*, for allowing me to incorporate in this Preface portions of articles which I have written for them. Also to Capt. W.J. Dowdy, both for singing shanties to me himself, and affording me facilities for interviewing inmates of the Royal Albert Institution, over which he presides. I also wish to express my gratitude to those sailors who have in recent years sung shanties to me, especially Capt. R.W. Robertson, Mr. Geo. Vickers, Mr. Richard Allen, of Seahouses, and Mr. F.B. Mayoss. And last, but not least, to Mr. Morley Roberts, who has not only sung shanties to me, but has also given me the benefit of his ripe nautical experience.

R.R.T.
Hampstead, 1921

NOTES ON THE SHANTIES

1. BILLY BOY

This is undoubtedly a coast song 'made into a shanty.' I heard it in Northumberland, both on shore and in ships, when I was a boy. The theme of a 'Boy Billy' seems common to folk-songs in different parts of the country. The tunes are different, and the words vary, but the topic is always the same: 'Billy' is asked where he has been all the day; he replies that he has been courting; he is then questioned as to the qualifications of his *inamorata* as a housewife. Dr. Vaughan-Williams' 'My Boy Billie' is in print and well known, as is also Mr. Cecil Sharp's 'My Boy Willie' ['English Folk-Songs,' vol. i, page 98]. I have also collected different versions in Warwickshire and Somerset. The version of line 1, page 3, bars 2 and 3, is older than the one given in my arrangement for male-voice chorus (Curwen Edition 50572), so, upon consideration, I decided to give it here. There are many more verses, but they are not printable, nor do they readily lend themselves to camouflage. The tune has not appeared in print until now.

2. BOUND FOR THE RIO GRANDE

The variants of this noble tune are legion. But this version, which a sailor uncle taught me, has been selected, as I think it the most beautiful of all. I used to notice, even as a boy, how it seemed to inspire the shantyman to sentimental flights of *Heimweh* that at times came perilously near poetry. The words of the well-known song, 'Where are you going to, my pretty maid?' were frequently sung to this shanty, and several sailors have told me that they had also used the words of the song known as 'The Fishes.' Capt. Whall gives 'The Fishes' on pages 96 and 97 of his book, and says that the words were, in his time, sometimes used to the tune of 'Blow the man down.'

3. GOOD-BYE, FARE YE WELL

This is one of the best beloved of shanties. So strongly did its sentiment appeal to sailors that one never heard the shantyman extemporize a coarse verse to it. Whall prints a version, page 71.

4. JOHNNY COME DOWN TO HILO

This is clearly of negro origin. I learnt several variants of it, but for its present form I am indebted to Capt. W.J. Dowdy.

5. CLEAR THE TRACK, LET THE BULLGINE RUN

The tune was a favorite in Yankee Packets. It does not appear in Whall. 'Bullgine' was American negro slang for 'engine.' I picked up this version in boyhood from Blyth seamen.

6. LOWLANDS

For another version see Whall (page 80), who says it is of American origin and comes from the cotton ports of the old Southern States. It was well known to every sailor down to the time of the China Clippers. My version is that of Capt. John Runciman, who belonged to that period. I have seldom found it known to sailors who took to the sea after the early seventies. The tune was sung in very free time and with great solemnity. It is almost impossible to reproduce in print the elusive subtlety of this haunting melody. In North-country ships the shantyman used to make much of the theme of a dead lover appearing in the night. There were seldom any rhymes, and the air was indescribably touching when humoured by a good hand. A 'hoosier,' by the way, is a cotton stevedore. An interesting point about this shanty is that, whether by accident or design, it exhibits a rhythmic device commonly practised by mediaeval composers, known as *proportio sesquialtera*. Expressed in modern notation it would mean the interpolation of bars of three-four time in the course of a composition which was in six-eight time. The number of quavers would, of course, be the same in each bar; but the rhythm would be different. The barring here adopted does not show this.

7. SALLY BROWN

For another version of this universally known shanty see Whall, page 64. Although its musical form is that of a halliard shanty, it was always used for the capstan. I never heard it used for any other purpose than heaving the anchor. The large-sized notes given in the last bar are those which most sailors sing to me nowadays; the small ones are those which I most frequently heard when a boy.

8. SANTY ANNA

This fine shanty was a great favorite, and in defiance of all history the sailor presents 'Santy Anna' in the light of an invariable victor. The truth is that Antonio Lopez de Santa Anna (1795-1876) was the last President of Mexico before the annexation by America of California, Texas, and New Mexico. He defeated the Spaniards at Zampico, and held Vera Cruz against the French, but was badly beaten at Molina del Rey by the United States Army under General Taylor (1847). He was recalled to the Presidency in 1853, but overthrown in 1855. He attempted to overturn the Republic in 1867; was captured and sentenced to death, but was pardoned on condition that he left the country. He retired to the United States until 1872, when a general amnesty allowed his return to Mexico. Like other Mexican Presidents, he lived a stormy life, but unlike most of them he died a natural death. Whall gives a version on page 89.

9. SHENANDOAH

This is one of the most famous of all shanties. I never met a sailor to whom it was unknown, nor have I ever found any two who sang it exactly alike. This version (sung to me by Capt. Robertson) is almost, but not quite, identical with the one I learnt as a boy. Shenandoah (English seamen usually pronounced it 'Shannandore') was a celebrated Indian chief after whom an American town is named. A branch of the Potomac river bears the same name. The tune was always sung with great feeling and in very free rhythm. Whall gives a version on page 1.

10. STORMALONG JOHN

This is one of the many shanties with 'Stormy' as their hero. Whatever other verses were extemporized, those relating to digging his grave with a silver spade, and lowering him down with a golden chain, were rarely omitted. Other favorite verses were:

> (a) I wish I was old Stormy's son.
> (b) I'd build a ship a thousand ton.

Who 'Stormy' was is undiscoverable, but more than a dozen shanties mourn him.

11. THE HOG'S-EYE MAN

Of the numberless versions of this shanty I have chosen that of Capt. Robertson as being the most representative. Of the infinite number of verses to this fine tune hardly one is printable. There has been much speculation as to the origin of the title. As a boy my curiosity was piqued by reticence, evasion, or declarations of ignorance, whenever I asked the meaning of the term. It was only in later life that I learnt it from Mr. Morley Roberts. His explanation made it clear why every *sailor* called it either 'hog-eye' or 'hog's-eye,' and why only *landsmen* editors ever get the word wrong. One collector labels the shanty 'The hog-eyed man,' and another goes still further wide of the mark by calling it 'The ox-eyed man.' The remarks on this shanty in the Preface will show the absurdity of both titles. That is all the explanation I am at liberty to give in print. Whall gives the shanty on page 118, his version differing but slightly from Capt. Robertson's.

12. THE WILD GOOSE SHANTY

This I learnt from Capt. John Runciman. Allusions to 'The Wild Goose Nation' occur in many shanties, but I never obtained any clue to the meaning (if any) of the term. The verse about 'huckleberry hunting' was rarely omitted, but I never heard that particular theme further developed. Whall gives another version (in six-eight time) on page 131.

13. WE'RE ALL BOUND TO GO

I used to hear this tune constantly on the Tyne. It is one of the few shanties which preserved a definite narrative, but each port seems to have offered variants on the names of the ships that were 'bound for Amerikee.' 'Mr. Tapscott' was the head of a famous line of emigrant ships. The last word in verse 5 was always pronounced *male*. This has led to many shantymen treating it not as *meal*, but as the *mail* which the ship carried. As the shanty is full of Irish allusions, the probabilities are that the word was *meal*, to which the sailor gave what he considered to be the Irish pronunciation. Whenever I heard the shanty it was given with an attempt at Irish pronunciation throughout. Capt. Whall (page 79) gives additional colour to the supposition that this was a general practice, for his version of verse 6 runs:

> Bad luck unto them *say*-boys,
> Bad luck to them I say;
> They broke into me *say*-chest
> And they stole me clothes away.

14. WHAT SHALL WE DO WITH THE DRUNKEN SAILOR?

This fine tune—in the first Mode—was always a great favorite. Although mostly used for windlass or capstan, Sir Walter Runciman tells me that he frequently sang to it for 'hand-over-hand' hauling. Whall gives it on page 107 under the title 'Early in the morning.' It is one of the few shanties that were sung in quick time.

15. BLOW, MY BULLY BOYS

This shanty has been included in every collection that I know of. (See Whall, page 91.) Most of my sailor relatives sang the last line thus:

Her masts and yards they shine like sil - ver.

Spotless decks, and 'masts and yards that shone like silver,' were the distinguishing marks of a Yankee Packet, and this immaculate condition was the result of a terrible discipline, in which the belaying pin was a gruesome factor.

16. BLOW THE MAN DOWN

This is the shanty which is perhaps the best known among landsmen. 'Winchester Street' is in South Shields, and in the old days was the aristocratic quarter where only persons of high distinction—such as shipowners, and 'Southspainer' skippers—lived. Whall gives the shanty on page 92.

17. CHEER'LY, MEN

This is a very well-known shanty, and the variants of it are endless. This particular version was sung to me by Capt. R.W. Robertson. It differs but slightly from the version which I originally learnt from Sir Walter Runciman. Very few of the words were printable, and old sailors who read my version will no doubt chuckle over the somewhat pointless continuation of the verses concerning Kitty Carson and Polly Riddle. They will, of course, see the point of my having supplied a Chopinesque accompaniment to such a shanty.

18. GOOD MORNING, LADIES ALL

The title belongs to other shanties as well; but, so far as I know, this tune has never been printed until now. I learnt it from Northumbrian sailors when a very small boy, and have never heard of its use in any other than Blyth and Tyne ships. It may be a Northumbrian air, but from such knowledge as I have gleaned of Northumbrian folk-tunes, I incline to the conjecture that it may have been picked up in more southern latitudes by some Northumbrian seaman.

19. HANGING JOHNNY

This cheery riot of gore is wedded to the most plaintive of tunes, and is immortalized by Masefield in his 'Sailor's Garland.' Nowadays one occasionally meets unhumorous longshore sailormen who endeavour to temper its fury to the shorn landsman by palming off a final verse, which gives one to understand that the previous stanzas have been only 'Johnny's' little fun, and which makes him bleat:

> They said I hanged for money,
> But I never hanged nobody.

I also possess a shanty collection where the words have so clearly shocked the editor that he has composed an entirely fresh set. These exhibit 'Johnny' as a spotless moralist, who would never *really* hang his parents, but would only operate (in a Pickwickian sense of course) on naughty and unworthy people:

> I'd hang a noted liar,
> I'd hang a bloated friar.
>
> I'd hang a brutal mother,
> I'd hang her and no other.
>
> I'd hang to make things jolly,
> I'd hang all wrong and folly.'

Imagine a shantyman (*farceur* as he ever was) making for edification in that style!

20. HILO SOMEBODY

This is another of the shanties I learnt as a boy from Blyth sailors, and which has never been printed before. I fancy that 'blackbird' and 'crew' must be a perversion of 'blackbird and *crow*,' as the latter figure of speech occurs in other shanties.

21. OH, RUN, LET THE BULLGINE RUN

The reference to the 'Bullgine' seems to suggest Transatlantic origin. There were endless verses, but no attempt at narrative beyond a recital of the names of places from which and to which they were 'running.' This version was sung to me by Mr. F.B. Mayoss, a seaman who sailed in the old China Clippers.

22. REUBEN RANZO

Alden gives this version, and I fancy it may have once been fairly general, as several of my relatives used to sing it. The version I mostly heard from other sailors, however, began:

Oh, pi-ty poor Reu-ben Ran-zo.

But from Mr. Morley Roberts I had the following:

Oh, pi-ty poor Reu-ben Ran-zo.

Capt. Robertson's version ran thus:

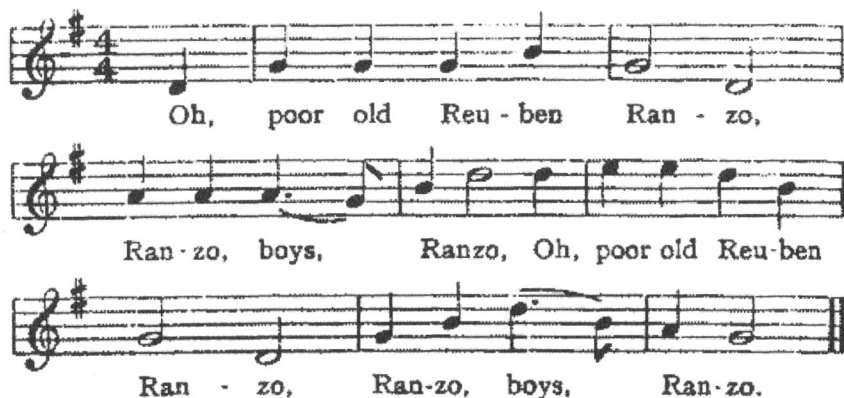

Oh, poor old Reu-ben Ran-zo,

Ran-zo, boys, Ranzo, Oh, poor old Reu-ben

Ran-zo, Ran-zo, boys, Ran-zo.

Whall gives another version on page 84.

Who Ranzo was must ever remain a mystery. Capt. Whall suggests that the word might be a corruption of Lorenzo, since Yankee Whalers took many Portuguese men from the Azores, where Lorenzo would have been a common enough name. He adds that in his time the shanty was always sung to the regulation words, and that 'when the story was finished there was no attempt at improvisation; the text was, I suppose, considered sacred.' He further says that he never heard any variation from the words which he gives.

I think he is right about the absence of improvisation on extraneous topics, but I used to hear a good deal of improvisation on the subject of Ranzo himself. I knew at least three endings of the story: (1) where the captain took him into the cabin, 'larned him navigation,' and eventually married him to his daughter; (2) where Ranzo's hatred of ablutions caused the indignant crew to throw him overboard; (3) where the story ended with the lashes received, not for his dirty habits, but for a theft:

> We gave him lashes thirty
> For stealin' the captain's turkey.

I have also heard many extemporaneous verses relating his adventures among the denizens of the deep after he was thrown overboard.

23. THE DEAD HORSE

This shanty was used both for hauling and for pumping ship. It seems to have had its origin in a rite which took place after the crew had 'worked off the dead horse.' The circumstances were these: Before any voyage, the crew received a month's pay in advance, which, needless to say, was spent ashore before the vessel sailed. Jack's first month on sea was therefore spent in clearing off his advance, which he called working off the dead horse. The end of that payless period was celebrated with a solemn ceremony: a mass of straw, or whatever other combustibles were to hand, was made up into a big bundle, which sometimes did, and more often did not, resemble a horse. This was dragged round the deck by all hands, the shanty being sung meanwhile. The perambulation completed, the dead horse was lighted and hauled up, usually to the main-yardarm, and when the flames had got a good hold, the rope was cut and the blazing mass fell into the sea, amid shouts of jubilation.

24. TOM'S GONE TO HILO

This beautiful tune was very popular. I have chosen the version sung to me by Mr. George Vickers, although in the first chorus it differs somewhat from the version I learnt as a boy:

A - way down Hi - lo.

It will be seen how closely the above resembles the version given by Whall on page 74. (It will be noted that he entitled it '*John's* gone to Hilo.') I give Mr. Vickers' verses about 'The Victory' and 'Trafalgar,' as I had never heard them sung by any other seaman. I have omitted the endless couplets containing the names of places to which Tommy is supposed to have travelled. As Capt. Whall says: 'A good shantyman would take Johnny all round the world to ports with three syllables, Montreal, Rio Grande Newfoundland, or any such as might occur to him.'

25. WHISKY JOHNNY

This Bacchanalian chant was a prime favorite. Every sailor knew it, and every collection includes some version of it.

26. BONEY WAS A WARRIOR

I never met a seaman who has not hoisted topsails to this shanty. Why Jack should have made a hero of Boney (he frequently pronounced it 'Bonny') is a mystery, except perhaps that, as a sailor, he realized the true desolation of imprisonment on a sea-girt island, and his sympathies went out to the lonely exile accordingly. Or it may have been the natural liking of the Briton for any enemy who proved himself a 'bonny fechter.'

27. JOHNNY BOKER

This popular shanty was sometimes used for bunting-up a sail, but more usually for 'sweating-up.' Although I have allowed the last note its full musical value, it was not prolonged in this manner aboard ship. As it coincided with the pull, it usually sounded more like a staccato grunt.

28. HAUL AWAY, JOE

The major version of this shanty (which appears in Part II) was more general in the last days of the sailing ship; but this minor version (certainly the most beautiful of them) is the one which I used to hear on the Tyne. The oldest of my sailor relatives never sang any other. This inclines me to the belief that it is the earlier version. The verses extemporized to this shanty were endless, but those concerning the Nigger Girl and King Louis never seem to have been omitted. As in No. 27, I have allowed the last note its full musical value, but aboard ship it was sung in the same manner as No. 27.

29. WE'LL HAUL THE BOWLIN'

This was the most popular shanty for 'sweating-up.' There are many variants of it. The present version I learnt from Capt. John Runciman. In this shanty no attempt was ever made to sing the last word. It was always shouted.

30. PADDY DOYLE'S BOOTS

This shanty differs from all others, as (a) it was sung *tutti* throughout; (b) it had only one verse, which was sung over and over again; and (c) it was used for one operation and one operation only, viz. bunting up the foresail or mainsail in furling. In this operation the canvas of the sail was folded intensively until it formed a smooth conical bundle. This was called a bunt, and a strong collective effort (at the word 'boots') was required to get it on to the yard.

Although the same verse was sung over and over again, very occasionally a different text would be substituted, which was treated in the same manner. Capt. Whall gives two alternatives, which were sometimes used:

> We'll all drink brandy and gin,

and—

> We'll all shave under the chin.

Mr. Morley Roberts also told me that a variant in his ship was—

> We'll all throw dirt at the cook.'

SHANTY SONGS
PART I

Billy Boy.

(NORTHUMBRIAN CAPSTAN SHANTY.)

SOLO.

1. Where hev ye been åål the day, Bil - ly Boy, Bil - ly Boy?

CHORUS.

Where hev ye been åål the day, me Bil - ly Boy?_____ I've been

SOLO.

walk - in' ààl the day —— With me charm-in' Nan-cy Grey. And me

Nan-cy kit - tl'd me fan-cy Oh me charm-in' Bil - ly Boy.

2. Is she fit to be yor wife
   Billy Boy, Billy Boy?
Is she fit to be yor wife, me Billy Boy?
   She's as fit to be me wife
   As the fork is to the knife
   And me Nancy, *etc.*

3. Can she cook a bit o' steak
   Billy Boy, Billy Boy?
Can she cook a bit o' steak, me Billy Boy?
   She can cook a bit o' steak,
   Aye, and myek a gairdle cake
   And me Nancy, *etc.*

4. Can she myek an Irish Stew
   Billy Boy, Billy Boy?
Can she myek an Irish Stew, me Billy Boy?
   She can myek an Irish Stew
   Aye, and "Singin' Hinnies" too.
   And me Nancy, *etc.*

Glossary:—

   ààl = all. Pronounced to rhyme with "shall" only the vowel must be very much more prolonged.
   kittled = tickled.
   myek = make.
   gairdle cake = girdle cake, i.e. a cake baked on a griddle.
   Singin' Hinnies — i.e. a species of Sally Lunn teacake only larger. Usually plentifully besprinkeld
                     with currants, in which case it is designated by pitmen as "Singin' Hinnies wi'
                     smàà co fizzors" (small coal fizzers.)

Bound for the Rio Grande.

(WINDLASS AND CAPSTAN SHANTY.)

1. I'll sing you a song of the fish of the sea. Oh_____ Ri - o._____ I'll sing you a song of the fish of the sea And we're

bound for the Ri - o Grande. Then a - way love, a - way,

'Way____ down Ri - o,____ So fare ye well my

allargando

VERSES 1 to 5. | LAST VERSE.
SOLO

pret - ty young gel. For we're bound for the Ri - o Grande. 2. Sing Grande.

allargando

2. Sing goodbye to Sally, and goodbye to Sue, Oh Rio, *etc.*
   And you who are listening, goodbye to you. And we're bound, *etc.*

3. Our ship went sailing out over the Bar
   And we pointed her nose for the South-er-en Star.

4. Farewell and adieu to you ladies of Spain
   And we're all of us coming to see you again.

5. I said farewell to Kitty my dear,
   And she waved her white hand as we passed the South Pier.

6. The oak, and the ash, and the bonny birk tree
   They're all growing green in the North Countrie.

Good-bye, fare ye well.

thought I heard the old man say Good-bye, fare ye well, Good-

2.   We're homeward bound, I hear the sound. *(twice)*

3.   We sailed away to Mobile Bay. *(twice)*

4.   But now we're bound for Portsmouth Town. *(twice)*

5.   And soon we'll be ashore again. *(twice)*

6.   I kissed my Kitty upon the pier
And it's oh to see you again my dear.

7.   We're homeward bound, and I hear the sound. *(twice)*

Johnny come down to Hilo.

(WINDLASS AND CAPSTAN.)

neb-ber see de like since I bin born, When a big buck nig-ger wid de

sea boots on, Says "Johnny come down to Hi-lo. Poor old

man." Oh wake her, oh, shake her, Oh wake dat gel wid de

VERSES 1 to 4. LAST
SOLO. VERSE.

blue dress on, When Johnny comes down to Hi-lo. Poor old man. 2. I man.

2. I lub a little gel across de sea,
    She's a Badian+ beauty and she sez to me.
                    "Oh Johnny," *etc.*

3. Oh was you ebber down in Mobile Bay?
    Where dey screws de cotton on a summer day.
                    When Johnny, *etc.*

4. Did you ebber see de ole Plantation Boss
    And de long-tailed filly and de big black hoss?
                    When Johnny, *etc.*

5. I nebber seen de like since I bin born
    When a big buck nigger wid de sea boots on.
                    Says "Johnny come down," *etc.*

+ *i.e.* Barbadian, to wit, a native of Barbados.

Clear the track, let the Bullgine run.

(WINDLASS AND CAPSTAN.)

smart-est clip-per you can find. Ah ho Way-oh, are you most done. Is the

Marget Evans of the Blue Cross Line. So clear the track, let the Bullgine run. Tib-by

Hey rig a jig in a jaunt-ing car. Ah ho Way-oh, are you most done. With Li - zer Lee all on my knee. So clear the track, let the Bull-gine run. 2. Oh the Bull-gine run.

2. Oh the Marget Evans of the Blue Cross Line
She's never a day behind her time.

3. Oh the gels are walking on the pier
And I'll soon be home to you, my dear.

4. Oh when I come home across the sea,
It's Lizer you will marry me.

5. Oh shake her, wake her, before we're gone;
Oh fetch that gel with the blue dress on.

6. Oh I thought I heard the skipper say
"We'll keep the brig three points away."

7. Oh the smartest clipper you can find
Is the Marget Evans of the Blue Cross Line.

Lowlands away.

(WINDLASS AND CAPSTAN.)

M. ♩ = 60.

Slowly, expressively, and in very free rhythm.

quasi recit.

SOLO.

(INTRODUCTION.) Low - lands,

a tempo

Low-lands, A - way my John, Low-lands, a - way,_____ I

a tempo

CHORUS.

SOLO.

heard them say, My dol - lar and a half a day. 1. A

dol-lar and a half a day is a Hoo-sier's pay.

CHORUS.

SOLO.

Lowlands, Lowlands, A - way my John. A dol-lar and a half a

CHORUS.

day_____ is ve-ry good pay. My dol-lar and a half a day.

SOLO.
2. Oh was you ev - er___ in___ Mo - bile Bay.
CHORUS.
Low-lands, Low-lands, A - way my John.
SOLO.
Screwing the cot - - ton by the day.
CHORUS.
My dol-lar and a half a day.

SOLO.

CHORUS.

3. All in the night my __ true love came. Low-lands,

Low-lands, a - way my John. All in the night __

CHORUS.

__ my true love came. My dol-lar and a half a day.

4. She came to me all in my sleep. *(twice)*

5. And her eyes were white my love. *(twice)*

6. And then I knew my love was dead. *(twice)*

- 33 -

Sally Brown.

(WINDLASS AND CAPSTAN.)

M. ♩ = 150.

SOLO.

1. Sal - - ly Brown she's a bright Mu - lat - ter.

2. Sally Brown she has a daughter
   Sent me sailin' 'cross the water.

3. Seven long years I courted Sally. *(twice)*

4. Sally Brown I'm bound to leave you
   Sally Brown I'll not deceive you.

5. Sally she's a 'Badian' beauty. *(twice)*

6. Sally lives on the old plantation
   She belongs the Wild Goose Nation.

7. Sally Brown is a bright Mulatter
   She drinks rum and chews terbacker.

Santy Anna.

(WINDLASS AND CAPSTAN.)

SOLO.

1. Oh   San - ty An - na   won the_ day.   Way -

CHORUS.

-Ah, me San - ty An - na.   Oh   San - ty An - na
won the day. All   on   the plains of Mex - i - co. 2. Oh   Mex - i - co.

2. He beat the Prooshans fairly, Way-Ah, *etc.*
   And whacked the British nearly. All on, *etc.*

3. He was a rorty gineral;
   A rorty snorty gineral.

4. They took him out and shot him.
   Oh when shall we forget him.

5. Oh Santy Anna won the day
   And Gin'ral Taylor run away.

Shenandoah.+

(WINDLASS AND CAPSTAN.)

Slowly and with much expression.

1. Oh Shenandoah, I long to hear you. A - way you rolling

+ The small notes in the piano part are to be played when there is no violin.

river. Oh Shenandoah, I long to hear you. A - way, I'm bound to

VERSES 1 to 5.   LAST VERSE.

go_____ 'Cross the wide Mis - sou - ri. 2. Oh - sou - ri.

2. Oh Shenandoah, I love your daughter. *(twice)*

3. 'Tis seven long years since last I see thee. *(twice)*

4. Oh Shenandoah, I took a notion
   To sail across the stormy ocean.

5. Oh Shenandoah, I'm bound to leave you.
   Oh Shenandoah, I'll not deceive you.

6. Oh Shenandoah, I long to hear you. *(twice)*

Stormalong John.

(WINDLASS AND CAPSTAN.)

Maestoso.
M. ♩ = 130.

SOLO.

1. Oh

CHORUS.

poor old Stor-my's dead and gone. Storm a - long boys,

2. I dug his grave with a silver spade. *(twice)*

3. I lower'd him down with a golden chain. *(twice)*

4. I carried him away to Mobile Bay. *(twice)*

5. Oh poor old Stormy's dead and gone. *(twice)*

The Hog's-eye Man.

(WINDLASS AND CAPSTAN.)

In leisurely fashion. M. ♩ = 88

SOLO.

1. Oh the hog's-eye man is the man for me, He were raised way down in Ten - ne - see. Oh hog's eye, oh.

.CHORUS.

Row the boat a-shore for the hog's-eye.__ Steady on a jig with a

hog's-eye oh, She wants the hog's-eye man. 2. Oh__ man.

VERSES 1 to 4.
SOLO.
LAST VERSE.

+2. Oh who's been here while I've been gone?
Some big buck nigger, with his sea boots on?

3. Oh bring me down my riding cane,
For I'm off to see my darling Jane.

4. Oh Jenny's in the garden a-picking peas,
And her golden hair's hanging down to her knees.

5. Oh a hog's-eye ship, and a hog's-eye crew,
And a hog's-eye mate, and a skipper too.

+ This verse was sometimes sung:—
"Now where have you been gone so long
You Yankee Jack wid de sea boots on?"

- 43 -

The Wild Goose Shanty.

(WINDLASS AND CAPSTAN.)

SOLO.

CHORUS.

1. I'm the Shan - ty - man of the Wild Goose Na - tion. Tib - by

SOLO.

Way - - ay ___ Hi - o - ha! I've left my ___ wife on a

CHORUS.

big ___ plan - ta - tion. ___ Hi - lo ___ my Ran - zo Hay!

2. Now a long farewell to the old plantation. *(twice)*

3. And a long farewell to the Wild Goose Nation. *(twice)*

4. Oh the boys and the girls went a huckleberry hunting. *(twice)*

5. Then good-bye and farewell you rolling river. *(twice)*

6. I'm the Shanty-man of the Wild Goose Nation.
   I've left my wife on a big plantation.

We're all bound to go.

(WINDLASS AND CAPSTAN.)

1. Oh John-ny was a ro-ver And to-day he sails a-way. Heave a-way,_____ my John-ny, Heave a-way_ _ _ay.____ Oh John-ny was a

ro - ver And to - day __ he sails a - way. Heave a -

VERSES 1 to 5. LAST VERSE.
SOLO.

- way __ my bul - ly boys, We're all bound to go. __ 2. As go. __

2. As I was walking out one day,
   Down by the Albert Dock.
                    Heave away, &c.
   I heard an emigrant Irish girl
   Conversing with Tapscott.
                    Heave away, &c.

3. "Good mornin', Mister Tapscott, sir,"
   "Good morn, my gel," sez he,
   "It's have you got a Packet Ship
   All bound for Amerikee?"

4. "Oh yes, I've got a Packet Ship,
   I *have* got one or two.
   I've got the *Jenny Walker*
   And I've got the *Kangeroo.*"

5. "I've got the *Jenny Walker*
   And to-day she does set sail,
   With five and fifty emigrants
   And a thousand bags o' male."+

6. Bad luck to thim Irish sailor boys,
   Bad luck to thim I say.   [bunk
   For they all got drunk, and broke into me
   And stole me clo'es away.

+ meal.

- 47 -

What shall we do
with the drunken sailor?

(WINDLASS AND CAPSTAN.)

SOLO.

1. What shall we do with the drunken sai-lor, What shall we do with the drunken sai-lor,

What shall we do with the drunk-en sai-lor · Ear-ly in the morn-ing?

CHORUS.

Hoo - ray and up she ri - ses, Hoo - ray and up she ri - ses,

Hoo - ray and up she ri - ses Ear-ly in the morn - ing.

2. Put him in the long-boat until he's sober. *(thrice)*

3. Pull out the plug and wet him all over. *(thrice)*

4. Put him in the scuppers with a hose-pipe on him. *(thrice)*

5. Heave him by the leg in a running bowlin'. *(thrice)*

6. Tie him to the taffrail when she's yard-arm under. *(thrice)*

Blow my bully boys.

(HALLIARD SHANTY.)

Yan - kee ship came down the ri - ver,   Blow,   boys

2. And how d'ye know she's a Yankee packet?
   The Stars and Stripes they fly above her.

3. And who d'ye think was skipper of her. *(twice)*

4. 'Twas Dandy Jim, the one-eyed nigger;
   'Twas Dandy Jim, with his bully figure.

5. And what d'ye think they had for dinner?
   Why bullock's lights and donkey's liver.

6. And what d'ye think they had for supper?
   Why weevilled bread and Yankee leather.

7. Then blow my boys, and blow together.
   And blow my boys for better weather.

8. A Yankee ship came down the river.
   Her masts and yards they shine like silver.

Blow the man down.

(HALLIARDS.)

M. ♩. = 88.

SOLO.

1. Oh —

CHORUS.

blow the man down, bul-lies, blow the man down.
o - ver the Bar on the thirteenth of May. } To me Way - ay,

SOLO.

CHORUS.

blow the man down. { Oh blow the man down, bul-lies, blow him a-way. }
{ The Gal-lop-er jumped, and the gale came a-way. }

Oh

VERSES 1 to 6. SOLO. LAST VERSE.

gimme some time to blow the man down. 2. We went blow the man down.

3. Oh the rags they was gone, and the chains they was jammed,
And the skipper sez he, "Let the weather be hanged."

4. As I was a-walking down Winchester Street,
A saucy young damsel I happened to meet.

5. I sez to her, "Polly, and how d'you do?"
Sez she, "None the better for seein' of you."

6. Oh, it's sailors is tinkers, and tailors is men.
And we're all of us coming to see you again.

7. So we'll blow the man up, and we'll blow the man down.
And we'll blow him away into Liverpool Town.

*Cheer'ly men.

(HALLIARDS.)

M. ♩. = 72.

(a la Chopin)

rall.

SOLO.   CHORUS.   SOLO.

1. Oh, Nancy Dawson, I - Oh.— Chee-lee men.   She robb'd the Bo'sun, I - Oh.—

a tempo

CHORUS.   SOLO.   CHORUS.

Chee-lee men.   That was a caution, I - Oh.   Chee-lee men.

* Pronounced "Chee-lee men."
⊕ If sung without accompaniment the portion within brackets may be omitted. If sung with accompaniment the note D (to the word "men") may be sung *crescendo* and held on to the end of the bar.

Oh   Haul - y,   I - Oh,____   Chee - lee   men.

AFTER LAST VERSE ONLY.

rall.

2. Oh Sally Racket. I-Oh, &c.
   Pawned my best jacket. I-Oh, &c.
   Sold the pawn ticket. I-Oh, &c.

3. Oh Kitty Carson
   Jilted the parson,
   Married a mason.

4. Oh Betsy Baker
   Lived in Long Acre,
   Married a quaker.

5. Oh Jenny Walker
   Married a hawker
   That was a corker.

6. Oh Polly Riddle
   Broke her new fiddle,
   Right through the middle.

Good morning, ladies all.

(HALLIARDS.)

Tenderly.

M. ♩. = 56.

SOLO.

1. Now a

CHORUS.

long good-bye to you, my dear, With a heave - oh

2. For we're outward bound to New York town;
                With a heave, *etc*.
And you'll wave to us till the sun goes down.
                And good morning, *etc*.

3. And when we get to New York town,
Oh it's there we'll drink, and sorrows drown.

4. When we're back once more in London Docks,
All the pretty girls will come in flocks.

5. And Poll, and Bet, and Sue will say:
"Oh it's here comes Jack with his three years' pay."

6. So a long good-bye to you, my dear,
And a last farewell, and a long farewell.

Hanging Johnny.

(HALLIARDS.)

With mock pathos.

M. ♩. = 72.

SOLO.

1. Oh they

call me hang - ing Johnny._____ A - way, boys, a-

CHORUS.

2. And first I hanged my daddy. *(twice)*

3. And then I hanged my mother,
   My sister and my brother.

4. And then I hanged my granny. *(twice)*

5. And then I hanged my Annie;
   I hanged her up +see canny.

6. We'll hang and haul together;
   We'll haul for better weather.

+ Northumbrian equivalent of "so nicely" or "so gently."

Hilo somebody.

(HALLIARDS AND INTERCHANGEABLE.)

With expression.
M. ♩ = 128.

SOLO.

1. The

CHORUS.

black - bird sang un - to our crew. Hi - lo boys,—

2. The blackbird sang so sweet to me. *(twice)*

3. We sailed away to Mobile Bay. *(twice)*

4. And now we're bound for London Town. *(twice)*

5. Then up aloft this yard must go. *(twice)*

6. I thought I heard the old man say:—
   "Just one more pull, and then belay."

7. Hooray my boys, we're homeward bound. *(twice)*

8. The blackbird sang unto our crew. *(twice)*

Oh run, let the Bullgine run.

(HALLIARDS.)

Brisk and lively.
M. ♩ = 150.

SOLO.

1. Oh we'll

CHORUS.

run all night till the morn - ing. Oh run, let the Bull - gine run. Way - yah,___ Oh - I - Oh,___

VERSES 1 to 8.   SOLO.   LAST VERSE.

run,   let   the Bull - gine   run.   2. Oh we   run.

2.   Oh we sailed all day to Mobile Bay.

3.   Oh we sailed all night across the Bight.[+]

4.   Oh we'll run from Dover to Cällis.

5.   Oh drive her captäin, drive her.

6.   Oh captain make her nose blood.

7.   She's a dandy packet and a flier too.

8.   With a dandy skipper, and a dandy crew.

9.   Oh we'll run all night till the morning.

+ Of Australia.

Reuben Ranzo.

(HALLIARDS.)

SOLO.   1. Oh poor old Reu - ben — Ran - - zo,   Oh   CHORUS.

2. Oh Ranzo was no sailor
   He shipped on board a whaler.

3. Old Ranzo couldn't steer her,
   Did you ever hear anything queerer?

4. Oh Ranzo was no beauty
   Why couldn't he do his duty?

5. Oh Ranzo washed once a fortnight
   He said it was his birthright.

6. They triced up this man so dirty
   And gave him five and thirty.+

7. Oh poor old Reuben Ranzo
   Ah pity poor Reuben Ranzo.

The dead horse.

(HALLIARDS, or PUMPING SHIP.)

poor old __ man came ri - ding by. And they

say so,   and they   hope so.   A   poor old— man came

ri - ding by.   Oh   poor   old   man.   ·2. I   man.

2.   I said "Old man your hoss will die." *(twice)*

3.   And if he dies I'll tan his skin. *(twice)*

4.   And if he lives you'll ride again. *(twice)*

5.   I thought I heard the skipper say. *(twice)*

6.   Oh one more pull and then belay. *(twice)*

7.   A poor old man came riding by. *(twice)*

Tom's gone to Hilo.

(HALLIARDS.)

Slowly and with expression.

M. ♩ = 72.

SOLO.

1. Tom - my's

gone and I'll go too,_____ A - way down

CHORUS.

2. Tommy's gone to Liverpool,
            Away, &c.
Oh, Tommy's gone to Liverpool,
        Tom's gone to Hilo.

3. Tommy's gone to Mobile Bay.
    Oh, Tommy's gone to Mobile Bay.

4. Tommy's gone, what shall I do?
    Oh, Tommy's gone, what shall I do?

5. Tommy fought at Tráfalgár.
    Oh, Tommy fought at Trafalgar.

6. The old Victory led the way.
    The brave old Victory led the way.

7. Tommy's gone for evermore.
    Oh, Tommy's gone for evermore.

Whisky Johnny.

(HALLIARDS.)

Incisively.
M. ♩ = 130.

SOLO.

CHORUS.

1. Oh whis-ky is the life of man. Whis-ky_____

2. Oh whisky makes me pawn my clothes.
   And whisky gàve me this red nose.

3. Oh whisky killed my poor old dad.
   And whisky druv my mother mad.

4. Oh whisky up, and whisky down.
   And whisky all around the town.

5. Oh whisky here, and whisky there.
   It's I'll have whisky everywhere.

6. Oh whisky is the life of man.
   It's whisky in an old tin can.

Boney was a warrior.

(HALLIARDS.)

2. Boney beat the Rooshians. *(twice)*

3. Boney beat the Prooshians. *(twice)*

4. Boney went to Möscow. *(twice)*

5. Moscow was a-fire. *(twice)*

6. Boney he came back again. *twice)*

7. Boney went to Elbow. *(twice)*

8. Boney went to Waterloo. *(twice)*

9. Boney was defeated. *(twice)*

10. Boney was a prisoner
    'Board the Billy Ruffian.*

11. Boney he was sent away,
    'Way to St. Helena.

12. Boney broke his heart, and died. *(twice)*

13. Boney was a warrior. *(twice)*

+ Francois.
* Sailor pronunciation of "Bellerophon."

Johnny Boker.

(FORE-SHEET.)

Strict time.
M. ♩ = 100. SOLO.

1. Oh do my Johnny Boker, Come rock and roll me o - ver.

CHORUS. | VERSES 1 to 9. SOLO. | LAST VERSE.

Do my Johnny Bo - ker, do. 2. Oh do.

2. Oh do my Johnny Boker,
The skipper is a rover.
Do my Johnny, &c.

3. Oh do, &c.
The mate he's never sober.
Do my, &c.

4. Oh do, &c.
The Bo'sun is a tailor.
Do my, &c.

5. Oh do, &c.
We'll all go on a jamboree.
Do my, &c.

6. Oh do, &c.
The Packet is a rollin'.
Do my, &c.

7. Oh do, &c.
We'll pull and haul together.
Do my, &c.

8. Oh do, &c.
We'll haul for better weather.
Do my, &c.

9. Oh do, &c. [Town.
And soon we'll be in London
Do my, &c.

10. Oh do, &c.
Come rock and roll me over.
Do my, &c.

Haul away Joe.

(FORE- SHEET.)

Andante molto.

M. ♩. = 52.

1. Way,— haul a - way,—— We'll haul a - way the bow - lin'.—

2. Way haul away. The packet is a-rollin'.

3. Way haul away. We'll hang and haul together.

4. Way haul away. We'll haul for better weather.

5. Once I had a nigger girl, and she was fat and lazy.

6. Then I had a Spanish girl, she nearly druv me crazy.

7. Geordie Charlton had a pig, and it was double jointed.

8. He took it to the blacksmith's shop to get its trotters pointed.

9. King Louis was the king o' France before the Revolution.

10. King Louis got his head cut off, and spoiled his Constitution.

11. Oh when I was a little boy and so my mother told me.

12. That if I didn't kiss the girls my lips would all go mouldy.

13. Oh once I had a scolding wife, she wasn't very civil.

14. I clapped a plaster on her mouth and sent her to the divvle.

We'll haul the bowlin'.

(FORE-SHEET.)

+ The last word ("haul") of the chorus is not sung but shouted *staccato*.

2. We'll haul the bowlin' for Kitty is my darlin'.

3. We'll haul the bowlin'; the fore-to-gallant bowlin'.

4. We'll haul the bowlin', the skipper is a growlin'.

5. We'll haul the bowlin', the packet is a rollin'.

6. We'll haul the bowlin' so early in the morning.

Paddy Doyle's boots.

(BUNT SHANTY.)

1. To my way - - ay - - ay - - ah, We'll
pay Pad-dy Doyle for his boots. To my boots.

Alternative verses.

2. We'll all throw dirt at the cook.

3. We'll all drink brandy and gin.

THE WAY OF THE SHIP
PART II

TO MY SON, PATRICK HUGH, WHO HAS ALREADY
ELECTED TO REVIVE THE FAMILY
TRADITION AND FOLLOW
THE SEA

INTRODUCTION
TO PART II

I am shortly publishing a historical and critical study of sea shanties, there is no necessity for this introduction to be other than brief.

During the five years which have elapsed since the publication of Part I there has been something of a boom in shanties. Old collections have been refurbished and put on the market again; new ones have appeared both in England and America. But when all has been said and done, Capt. W. B. Whall's *Sea Songs, Ships, and Shanties* still maintains its pre-eminence as the one authoritative book on the subject—the one and only book in which a sailor will find nothing erroneous or even disputable.

With the exception of Joanna C. Colcord's *Roll and Go* (published last year), the American collections are compilations from other people's work. But Miss Colcord speaks with the authority of one who was born at sea in the cabin of a sailing ship of which her father was captain. She claims descent from five generations of deep-water seamen. She spent the first eighteen years of her life in her father's ship, sailing with him on China voyages, 'knowing none but seamen, seeing nothing but ships, and ports and oceans.' Her book will prove even more useful when it is purged of the inaccuracies which seem to indicate hasty or careless preparation for the press. I note two examples since they concern myself (they are typical of the rest).

On page 23, she says:

Perhaps some idea of the difficulties in the way of the collector of shanties may be gained from the fact that this same shanty appears in the Tozer collection under the name 'The Chanty-Man's Song', the first line being 'I'm chanty-man of the working party', in Bullen's as 'Oh, what did you give for your fine leg of mutton?' and in Terry's as 'The Wild Goose Shanty', bringing in the mysterious 'Wild Goose Nation' which recurs in several British shanties. All of these versions use practically the same chorus; but none makes mention of the quest for huckleberries.

The answer to this is that not only do Whall, Bullen, Sharp, and myself include the 'huckleberry' verse, but in my 'Notes on the Shanties' in Part I of this collection, I wrote (page xiv) 'the verse about huckleberry hunting was rarely omitted.'

Again (on page 9)—speaking of 'The Black Ball Line' shanty—she says:

As happened to so many of the old shanties, this one was modernized in later years; and the version given by Terry works a ship from Liverpool to Mobile and brings her back loaded with cotton—a voyage no Blackballer ever made.

The answer to this is that my version of 'The Black Ball Line' is now printed for the first time in this volume. By what species of clairvoyance Miss Colcord could scent inaccuracy in a version nearly two years before it was published beats me entirely. As a matter of fact, the version which makes a Blackballer perform so remarkable a voyage will be found on page 26 of Sharp's *English Folk Chanteys*.

Of the English collections published during the past five years, the one which is not a compilation from printed sources is *Six Sea Shanties*, by A. Whitehead and Taylor Harris, published by Messrs. Boosey and Co., in which the authors have taken their tunes down from the actual singing of a seaman.

One feature of this volume (which was absent from Part I) is the capstan shanties which were nothing more than popular songs fitted with new words. Folk-song enthusiasts may object to this, but it is obvious that no collection of shanties could be considered representative which excluded tunes so universally employed at sea as 'John Brown's body', 'The Banks of Sacramento', 'Can't you dance the polka?', etc.

R. R. TERRY
Woodstock, July, 1926

NOTES ON THE SHANTIES

31. THE BLACK BALL LINE

This is one of the best known of the older shanties, and some form of it appears in nearly every collection. Strangely enough, Capt. Whall does not include it in his Sea Songs, Ships, and Shanties. The version which appears here was sung to me by Mr. Geo. Vickers, in 1914.

32. ONE MORE DAY

This was a homeward-bound shanty in which all the grievances of the voyage were ventilated. It was known to every sailor. The lugubrious manner of its rendering seemed in strange contrast with the elation one expected on nearing port. Whall gives a version on page 77.

33. A-ROVING. I.

I learnt this version from Mr. Jas. Runciman. It differs but little from the usual one found in *The Scottish Students' Song Book* and similar publications. Whall gives a version on page 81.

34. A-ROVING. II.

This version was sung to me by Mr. Short at Watchet, Somerset. There is another version in print (which differs at several points) taken down from his singing. This only goes to prove (what every collector of shanties knows) that shantymen are given to varying their versions according to the mood of the moment.

35. THE BANKS OF SACRAMENTO

This will be recognized as a variant of Stephen Foster's American 'nigger' song, 'Camptown Races' (better known as 'Doodah-doodah-day'), but whether Foster got his tune from the shanty or vice versa must remain a moot point. Miss C. Fox-Smith (the well known nautical authoress) says: 'As a matter of fact, it is a question which of the two (i.e. the song or the shanty) is the older. "The Banks of Sacramento" certainly dates from the late 'forties or early 'fifties; whether "Camptown Races" came earlier than that I cannot say, but I should doubt it.' A biography of Foster gives 1850 as the date of his song, and although this does not preclude the possibility of the shanty being older than the song, neither does it establish it. It is worth asking, however, that if the sailor (always ready as he was to adapt any shore song as a shanty) did seize on 'Camptown Races' because of its amazing popularity, why did he not seize on any other songs of Foster ('Swanee River' for instance) which had a greater vogue and were equally adaptable as shanties?

Whall gives a version on page 65

36. THE SHAVER

I learnt this shanty from the singing of the late Mr. James Runciman, who told me that he learnt it from a relative who was a great uncle of mine. It has the same tune as the shanty, 'Poor Paddy works on the railway.' Bullen and others have rejected 'Poor Paddy' on the ground that it was a Christy Minstrel song, and not a real shanty. This is doubtless true as regards the words. But—according to my great uncle—the tune was sung at sea (to the words of 'The Shaver') before the Christy Minstrels came into existence. Only the first two verses of this shanty are possible in their original form.

37. PADDY WORKS ON THE RAILWAY

This form of the shanty is the best-known amongst sailors. The shantyman always began with 'eighteen hundred and forty-one' and took the following years seriatim in successive verses. This shanty differed from most others in as much as the couplets always rhymed, and the tune varied less (in the hands of different shantymen) than any other I know. The present words are all from Mr. Short's singing. They are very much like those given by Whall (page 88).

38. CAN'T YOU DANCE THE POLKA?

This was a prime favourite in the palmy days of the sailing vessel. Every sailor knew it. Whall gives a version on Page 65, from which the present solo verses are taken, but the tune (which differs at many points from Capt. Whall's version) is the version sung to me in 1914 by Capt. Robertson.

In childhood I have heard the last lines of the chorus as:

> 'Oh, you New York gels,
> I love you for your money.'

Since 'money' rhymes with 'honey', and 'polka' does not, I am still wondering which was the original.

39. JOHN BROWN'S BODY

The history of this song has often been told and needs no repetition. For the British sailor it had none of the associations that it held for Americans. The British sailor liked the tune and 'made it into a shanty' which became one of the most popular in his repertory. The words were distinctly ribald, but one must remember that to him 'John Brown' was no more than a figure of speech, as abstract as 'Reuben Ranzo.' The shantyman's historical irrelevancy is seen in verse 2, where 'John Brown' is substituted for 'Jeff Davis' of the original, and the sentence is put into the past tense. The present version was sung to me by Capt. Robertson, but I have rarely met a sailor who did not know some form of it. When the sailor took a shore melody he never debased it; his alterations were usually improvements, and I think this is a case in point.

40. WHOOP JAMBOREE

I have never heard this shanty from anyone save Mr. Short. A version of it, taken down from his singing, has already appeared in print under the title 'Whip Jamboree.' The word as 'coughed up' by Mr. Short (with a shock of the glottis) sounded more like 'Whup.' The printed version gives

Jam-bo - ree

but I have set down the actual notes sung by Mr. Short to me. The same version gives three verses; I have set down the four which Mr. Short sang.

41. MY JOHNNY

I never heard this shanty save from Mr. Jas. Runciman, and should have set it down as a shore song but for his telling me that he had heard it as a: shanty. The words are of the sentimental type beloved of sailors, and the tune is redolent of the Venetian gondola, and the tinkling guitar with its persistent tonic and dominant harmonies (which last I have done my best to avoid).

42. THE DRUMMER AND THE COOK

This is obviously a music-hall song taken over wholesale. I learnt it from Capt. John Runciman, who in turn had it from the cook of the Blyth brig *Northumberland*, in which vessel it was used as a shanty. I remember nothing of this cook except that he was called 'Alf', and that (as was sometimes the case in ships with small crews) he acted as shantyman in the *Northumberland*. As Capt. John Runciman (who used to sing the whole song) is dead, and as neither Sir Walter Runciman (who also knew it in his youth) nor myself can now remember more than the first verse, I have been guilty of writing the remaining ones which here appear.

N.B. There were two Blyth brigs called *Northumberland*. The first (172 tons) was built at Perth in 1859; the second (271 tons) was built at Blyth in 1862. Information concerning both vessels occurs in Sir Walter Runciman's book Collier Brigs and their Sailors. It was in the larger of the two that 'Alf' sailed.

43. MISS LUCY LONG

This was sung to me by Mr. Short. I have never heard it from anyone else.

44. DO LET ME GO, GIRLS

This also was sung to me by Mr. Short. As he had only one verse of words, I have perpetrated the remaining two.

45. BLOW, YE WINDS OF MORNING

This shanty is peculiar. It is the only example I have met of a sea song being used as a shanty. Shore songs were annexed wholesale, but the sailor was rigid in banning sea songs for shantying purposes. But Mr. Short, who sang this version to me, assured me that it was used as a shanty in his ship. To my mind, his tune is an improvement on the original, for which see Whall, page 35. Capt. Whall adds the information that it was a song of the midshipman's berth rather than the forecastle, and as he served as midshipman in the Blackwall frigates, he, speaks with authority on the point. Mr. Short's words resemble the originals only in the first verse.

46. FIRE DOWN BELOW

This was a shanty known to almost every sailor who had ever worked at the pumps. It had endless verses, most of which I have long forgotten. The authoress of Roll and Go describes it well: 'Pumping ship was a long, monotonous spell of hard work unless enlivened by a song. Almost any of the capstan shanties could be used on the pump-brakes, but a few (this one among them) were kept by the force of convention for no other use. Jack would have his joke, even about that most dreaded of dangers-fire at sea; and the joke lay in his choosing non-inflammable portions of the ship in which to locate his imaginary fire. There is always, of course, a fire in the galley, which is the ship's kitchen.'

47. SHALLOW BROWN

This beautiful shanty was a general favorite, and the present version is the one sung by all my sailor relatives. It differs very slightly from that given by Whall, page 119.

48. A LONG TIME AGO

This was another well-known shanty. The version is that sung to me by Mr. Geo. Vickers. As verse 2 never seemed to be omitted, it points to the shanty being of American origin. Masefield quotes a version of the words in A Sailor's Garland, but in place of Mr. Vicker's 'family' who 'lived on a hill: he puts the Yankee Packet:

>She was waiting for a fair wind to get under way,
>If she hasn't had a fair wind she's lying there still.

In fact, at this point, every version had a verse concerning some person (or persons) or thing that was static if certain named conditions were not fulfilled. One, sent me by an old sailor began:

>'There once was a farmer in Norfolk did dwell'

As his rhyme for 'dwell' happened to be 'hell', it is easy to see what alternatIve dwellings were open to the farmer.

49. WON'T YOU GO MY WAY

This charming shanty was sung to me by Mr. Short. I have not met any other sailor who knows it. A version (differing from the present one in the music of bar 9, and the words of verses five and six) is given in C. J. Sharp's collection, taken down from Mr. Short's singing, also. Mr. Short may have exercised the shantyman's privilege of varying melody or words at will. ,At any rate, I have set both down as he sang them to me.

50. HILO JOHN BROWN

Whall gives a version of this (p. 85) under the title, 'Stand to your ground', in which the words differ only slightly from those I have heard. As my version of the tune is an inferior one I am enabled, by the kind permission of Capt. Whall's executors, to reproduce his melody with one difference: Capt. Whall gives a G sharp in bars 2 and 3 of the last line, and this is, no doubt, the way it was sung at sea in his time. But the tune is not in a minor key but in the First Mode. I have, therefore, eliminated the G sharp. I feel justified in this course because—although I have met only two seamen who knew the shanty, both sang the chorus with the G natural.

51. ROLL THE COTTON DOWN

This was known to every seaman who had been in the cotton trade. All my sailor relatives sang some form of it. The present version is that of Capt. John Runciman. It is clearly of American origin.

52. ROUND THE CORNER SALLY

I have not heard anyone save Mr. Short sing this shanty. The first verse, as I took it down from him, had three lines for the soloist. As I knew of only one other hauling shanty with this peculiarity ('Cheer'ly men') I bided my time until Mr. Short had sung other verses. I then found that these verses were in couplets (the usual hauling form). I have, therefore, adhered to the couplet form throughout.

53. THE BULLY BOAT IS COMING

This was sung to me by Mr. Short. His words run, 'Don't you hear the paddles rolling', but Mr. Mayoss, Mr. Allen, and others always sang 'paddles roaring', which seems the more probable reading.

I suspect 'Rando' ought to have been 'Ranzo', but as Mr. Short sang the former word, I have set it down here.

54. MY TOMMY'S GONE AWAY

This is a variant of the sentiment of 'Tom's gone to Hilo' (see Part I) but the tune is different and not so good. The version is that of Mr. Short.

55. SING FARE YOU WELL

This was also sung to me by Mr. Short. I had not heard it before, nor does it appear in any other collection.

56. O BILLY RILEY

Sung to me by Mr. Short. I have not found any other sailor who knows it.

57. TIME FOR US TO LEAVE HER

The original words (for which see Whall, p. 68) date from the 'fifties, and referred to the Irish emigrants whom the old packet-ships carried to America. They soon fell into disuse, and the shanty was used for ventilating grievances when nearing a home port. The tune was known to every sailor, and appears in most collections in one form or another. It's use seems to have been confined to British ships. I have as yet found no trace of its being used in American vessels. For further information see Whall, page 68.

58. LIZER LEE

Sung to me by Mr. Short. It is a better version than those sung by Sir Walter Runciman and others. The best version I know is the printed one by Frank Bullen, but as I never heard Mr. Bullen sing it (and in this book I have set down no tune which has not actually been sung to me by some sailor) I have done 'the next best thing' and given Mr. Short's version. Bullen's capital tune runs thus:

Oh, you Li - zer Lee. Yan-kee John, storm a - long.

Li - zer Lee is de gel for me. Yan-ke e John, storm a - long.

59. A HUNDRED YEARS ON THE EASTERN SHORE

Some form of this was known to nearly every British seaman. The present version was sung to me by Mr. Geo. Vickers. Joanna C. Colcord (in her book, Roll and Go) states (I do not know on what authority) that it is 'the only shanty which can be identified with the Baltimore clippers.' She gives four additional stanzas, which I do not include here, as I have not heard any British seaman sing them. They were sung in American vessels, however.

60. WALK HIM ALONG, JOHNNY

I have heard no one sing this save Mr. Short. The tune differs at several points (notably, bars 6 and 7, page 59) from C. J. Sharp's printed version taken down from Mr. Short. But I have set it down exactly as he sang it to me.

61. HILONDAY

I learned this in boyhood from the late Mr. James Runciman. I do not know in which ship he picked it up, but one of my earliest recollections is hearing him and W. E. Henley give tongue to it at the house of the latter (in the days when he lived at Shepherd's Bush— then an outlying suburb). Henley's knowledge of the sea (like R. L. Stevenson's) was the acquired knowledge of the literary landsman, but shanties—especially the grim ones—had a special appeal for him, and he was fond of singing them. The sea song, 'Time for us to go', which he incorporated in the play of Admiral Guinea (calling it a 'chanty') I learnt from him in my boyhood, to a tune which I understood was his own composition. It is a good imitation of a capstan shanty, but I do not include it in this collection as it was never sung at sea; I hope one day to publish it separately.

62. STORMALONG

This (like No. 10 in Part I) is one of the many shanties which mourn the mythical hero 'Stormy.' It is the one which was the most popular, and every seaman knew it. The present version is that of Sir Walter Runciman. Whall gives a version on page 87.

63. SO HANDY, MY GELS

Sung to me by Mr. Short, Mr. Morley Roberts, and most other sailors of my acquaintance. See also Whall, page 128.

64. THE SAILOR LIKES HIS BOTTLE, O

Although I have known this shanty almost as long as I can remember, I have never heard it aboard ship, and so I do not pretend to explain how the first line was manipulated. At the moment of writing I cannot get in touch with the particular seamen whom I know could enlighten me. Rather than delay the publication of this collection I will hold the matter over, and publish the result of my inquiries in my forthcoming book (referred to in the introduction) on the shanty.

65. HAUL AWAY, JOE

This major version of the fine minor tune in Part I (page 56) was almost equally popular. I noted that Sir Walter Runciman, and most of the older generation of seamen· always sang the minor version. The major one was mainly confined to a younger generation, but Whall gives it on page 117.

SHANTY SONGS
PART II

The Black Ball Line.

(CAPSTAN.)

VOICE.

M. ♩ = 132.

SOLO.

1. In the

PIANO.

Ped. ✳ Ped. ✳

CHORUS.

3

Black Ball Line I served my time. A - way - ay - ay, Hoo-

Ped. ✳ Ped. ✳ Ped. ✳

2. It'll carry you along through frost and snow,
   And take you where the wind don't blow.

3. At Liverpool Docks I bade adieu
   To Poll and Bet, and lovely Sue.

4. And now we're bound for New York Town,
   It's there we'll drink, and sorrow drown.

5. It's there I'll sport my long-tailed blue. *(twice)*

One more day.

(CAPSTAN.)

M. ♩ = 80.

SOLO.

1. On - ly one more day, my John - ny,

2. Only one more day, my Johnny;
     One more day.
   We'll cross the bar to-morrow,
     One more day.
       (Repeat whole of first verse as chorus.)

3. Don't you hear the old man roarin', Johnny,
     One more day?
   Don't you hear that pilot bawlin',
     One more day?
         (Repeat first verse as before.)

4. Can't you hear those gals a-callin', Johnny,
     One more day?
   Can't you hear the capstan pawlin',
     One more day?
         (Repeat first verse as before)

A-Roving. I.

(CAPSTAN.)

Am-ster-dam there lived a maid, Mark well what I do say. In

Am-ster-dam there lived a maid, And she was mis-tress of her trade. I'll

CHORUS.

go no more a-rov-ing with you, fair maid. A-rov-ing, a-rov-ing, Since rov-ing's been my ru-i-in, I'll go no more a-rov-ing with you, fair maid. (2) I maid.

VERSES 1 to 3. SOLO | LAST VERSE

2. I took that fair maid for a walk.
          Mark well, *etc.*
I took that fair maid for a walk.
And we had such a loving talk.
          I'll go no more, *etc.*

3. I put my arm around her waist.
          Mark well *etc.*
I put my arm around her waist,
So slim, and trim, and tightly laced.
          I'll go no more *etc.*

4. I took that maid upon my knee.
          Mark well, *etc.*
I took that maid upon my knee.
Said she, "Give over! Let me be!"
          I'll go no more, *etc.*

A-roving. II.

(CAPSTAN.)

lived a maid, And she was mis-tress of the trade I'll go no more a -

CHORUS.

-rov-ing with you, false maid. A - rov - ing, a - rov - ing, Since roving's been my

VERSES 1 to 8. | LAST VERSE.
SOLO.

ru - i - in, I'll go no more a - rov-ing with you, false maid. 2. I maid.

2. I took this fair maid for a walk,
    Bless you etc.
    And we had such a loving talk.
    I'll go no more etc.

3. I took her hand within my own,
    And said "I'm bound for my old home."

4. In Plymouth Town there lived a maid,
    And she was mistress of the trade.

The banks of Sacramento.

(CAPSTAN.)

M. ♩ = 80.

SOLO.

CHORUS.

1. Bos-ton ci - ty is a - fire. With a

hoo-dah, and a doo-dah.

SOLO.

Bos - ton ci - ty is a - fire,

CHORUS.

Hoo - dah, doo - dah day. Blow boys___ blow, for

Cal - i - for - nye - o. There's plen - ty of gold so

VERSES 1 to 3.   SOLO.   LAST VERSE.

I've been told, On the banks of Sa - cra - men-to. 2. We're -men-to.

2. We're bound away at the break of day. *(twice)*

3. The rose is red; the violet's blue;

O Amble girls we all love you.

4. Sally Brown she's come to town.

Sally Brown's got a new silk gown.

The Shaver.

(CAPSTAN.)

sha - ver, a sha - ver. Oh I was wea - ry

of the sea, When I___ was just a sha - ver. 2.O they sha - ver.

VERSES 1 to 3.
SOLO.

LAST VERSE.

2. O they whacked me up, and they whacked me down;
    The mate he cracked me on the crown;
    They whacked me round and round and round,
                    When I was, *etc.*

3. When I went aloft by the lubber's hole,
    The mate he cried "O dang yer soul,
    It's the futtock shrouds is the way yer bound,"
                    When I was, *etc.*

4. When we lollop'd around about Cape Horn,
    I wished that I had never been born,
    And I wished I was home all safe and sound,
                    When I was, *etc.*

Paddy works on the railway.*

(CAPSTAN.)

Lyrics under the staves:

1. In eight - een hun-dred and for - ty one, My cor - du - roy breech - es I put on. With a stick in my fist, a - bout two foot long, To work up - on the

*A "Christy Minstrel" version of the music of the preceding. See notes on the Shanties.

rail - way, the rail - way. I'm wear - ied of the

VERSES 1 to 6. SOLO. | LAST VERSE.

rail - way. O poor Pad-dy works on the rail - way. 2. In rail - way.

2. In eighteen hundred and forty two
I did not know what I should do.
And I resolved to put her through
    To work, *etc.*

3. In eighteen hundred and forty three
I paid my passage across the sea,
To New York, and Amerikee
    To work, *etc.*

4. In eighteen hundred and forty four
I landed on the American shore,
And never to return no more
    To work, *etc.*

5. In eighteen hundred and forty five
Things looked pretty well alive,
And I thought to myself I'd strive
    To work, *etc.*

6. In eighteen hundred and forty six,
When I was in a terrible fix,
I thought to myself I'd take my sticks,
    To work, *etc.*

7. I had a sister, her name was Grace,
Bad cess unto her ugly face,
She brought me to a deep disgrace
    A-working, *etc.*

Can't you dance the Polka.

(CAPSTAN.)

-way   you san - ty,   My   dear   ho - ney.___

O   you New York gels,   Can't you dance the pol - ka. 2. To   pol - ka.

VERSES 1 to 3.   LAST VERSE.
SOLO.

2. To Tiffany's I took her,
        I did not mind expense;
    I bought her two gold earrings,
        And they cost me fifty cents.
                    Then away, *etc.*

3. Says she "You lime-juice sailor,
        Now see me home you may."
    But when we reached her cottage door
        She unto me did say —
                    Then away, *etc.*

4. My flash man he is a Yankee,
        With his hair cut short behind;
    He wears a tarry jumper,
        And he sails in the Black Ball Line.
                    Then away, *etc.*

John Brown's body.

(CAPSTAN.)

2. We hanged John Brown upon a sour apple tree *(thrice)*

3. John Brown's wife has got a wart upon her nose *(thrice)*

4. John Brown's daughter chews terbacker by the pound *(thrice)*

5. John Brown's baby is a yankee-doodle-doo *(thrice)*

6. John Brown's body lays a-mould'ring in the grave *(thrice)*

Whoop Jamboree.

(CAPSTAN.)

1. Now, my lads, be of good cheer, For the I-rish land will soon draw near. In a few days more we'll sight Cape Clear. O

CHORUS.

Jen-ny, get your oat - cake done. Whoop jam - bo-ree, whoop

jam - bo - ree, Oh you long - tailed black man, poke it up be-hind. Whoop

jam - bo - ree, whoop jam - bo - ree, O Jen-ny, get your oat-cake done.

2. Now Cape Clear it is in sight,
  We'll be off Holyhead by to-morrow night;
  And we'll shape our course for the Rock Light,
  O Jenny, *etc.*

3. Now, my lads, we're round the Rock,
  All hammocks lashed and chests all locked.
  We'll haul her into the Waterloo dock.
  O Jenny, *etc.*

4. Now, my lads, we're all in dock,
  We'll be off to Dan Lowrie's on the spot;
  And now we'll have a good roundabout.
  O Jenny, *etc.*

My Johnny.

(CAPSTAN.)

Slowly. M. ♩. = 66.

SOLO.

1. We're homeward bound to-

-day,— But where is my Johnny?— My own dear Johnny,— My own dear

CHORUS.

SOLO.

Johnny.— We'll drink and court and play,— But al-ways think of Johnny.— My live - ly

CHORUS.

L.H.   L.H.   L.H.

SOLO.

Johnny, good-bye.___ In the mid-dle of the sea___ my boy is float-ing free,___ So

CHORUS.

far___ a-way from me,___ So far___ a-way from me ___ In the mid-dle of the sea ___ My

SOLO.

AFTER VERSE 1. | AFTER VERSE 2.

boy is floating free,___ So far___ away from me,___ my love. (2.) So love.___

2. So gay we went away,
   Me and my pretty Johnny,
      My own dear Johnny, *etc.*
   But where is he to-day?
   O always think of Johnny.
      ♪ My lively Johnny, good-bye.
   'Twas just by Finisterre
   Where the birds are free in the air,
   We buried Johnny there,
   We buried Johnny there,
      In the middle of the sea, *etc.*

The drummer and the cook.

(CAPSTAN.)

M. ♩ = 168.

SOLO.

1. Oh there was a lit-tle drummer and he loved a one-eyed cook. And he

loved her, O he loved her though she had a cock-eyed look, With her

CHORUS.

one eye in the pot, And the t'oth-er up the chim-ney, With a

VERSES 1 to 6. | LAST VERSE.

SOLO.

Bow-wow-wow, Fal-lal the dow-a-did-dy Bow-wow-wow. When this Bow-wow-wow

2. When this couple went a-courtin' for to walk along the shore,
   Sez the drummer to the cookie, "You're the gel that I adore."

3. When this couple went a-courtin', for to walk along the pier,
   Sez the cookie to the drummer "An' I love you too, my dear."

4. Sez the drummer to the cookie, "Aint the weather fine to-day?"
   Sez the cookie to the drummer, "Is that all ye got to say?"

5. Sez the drummer to the cookie, "Will I buy the weddin' ring?"
   Sez the cookie "Now you're talkin'. That would be the very thing."

6. Sez the drummer to the cookie, "Will ye name the weddin' day?"
   Sez the cookie, "We'll be married in the merry month o' May."

7. When they went to church to say "I will", the drummer got a nark*
   For her one eye gliffed⁺ the Parson, and the t'other killed the Clerk.

*Nark = a disagreeable surprise caused by a *person*, not by a circumstance.

⁺To gliff = to frighten.

Miss Lucy Long.

(CAPSTAN.)

M. ♩.= 68.   SOLO.

1. Was you ev - er on — the Brum - a - low, Where the Yan - kee boys are all the go? To me way ay___ ay, ___ Ha Ha___ me

CHORUS.

Johnny boys, Ha, Ha, ___ why ___ don't you

try for to ring Miss Lucy Long? 2. O as Long.

VERSES 1 to 3. SOLO.

LAST VERSE.

2. O! as I walked out one morning fair,
   To view the views and take the air
                    To me way *etc.*

3. 'Twas there I met Miss Lucy fair;
   'Twas there we met I do declare.
                    To me way *etc.*

4. I rung her all night and I rung her all day,
   And I rung her before she went away.
                    To me way *etc.*

Do let me go, girls.

(CAPSTAN.)

SOLO.

1. It's of a mer-chant's daugh-ter be-longed to Cal-la-o. ___ Hoo-raw ___ my yal-ler gels doo-dle let me go.

Doo - dle let me go____ gels, Doo - dle let me

go._____ Hoo - raw____ my yal - ler gels,

VERSES 1 and 2.   SOLO. AFTER LAST VERSE.

doo - dle let me go.___ 2. A - doo - dle let me go.___

2. A-courting of the maiden came a sailor long ago.

3. But he left her broken-hearted on the shores of Callao.

*Blow, ye winds of morning.

(CAPSTAN.)

I walked out one morn-ing fair To view the meadows round, It's

there I spied a maid-en fair Come trip-ping o'er the ground. O___

*This is the only instance- in my experience- of a Sea Song being adapted and used as a Shanty. [Ed.]

blow, ye winds of morn-ing, Blow, ye winds, Hi! Ho!

Clear a-way the morn-ing dew, And blow— boys blow. (2.) My blow.

VERSES 1 to 5. | LAST VERSE.
SOLO.

2. My father has a milk-white steed.
   And he is in the stall.
   He will not eat his hay or corn,
   Nor will not go at all.

3. When we goes in a farmer's yard
   And sees a flock of geese,
   We dang their eyes and cuss their thighs
   And knock down five or six.

4. As I was a walking
   Down by the riverside
   It's there I saw a lady fair
   A-bathing in the tide.

5. As I was a-walking
   Out by the moonlight,
   It's there I saw a yeller gel,
   And her eyes they shone so bright.

6. As I was a-walking
   Down Paradise Street,
   It's there I met old John de Goss,*
   He said "Will you stand treat?"

* The reference is not to the famous baritone singer, but to a Liverpool shipowner of last century (with the shellback's mispronunciation of his name, of course).

Fire down below.

(PUMPING-SHIP SHANTY.)

CHORUS.

Fire, _____ fire, _____ fire down be - low, _____ It's
fetch a buck - et o' wa - ter girls, there's fire down be - low.

2. Fire in the fore-top, fire in the main;
   It's fetch a bucket o' water girls, and put it out again.

3. Fire in the fore-peak, fire down below;
   It's fetch a bucket o' water girls, there's fire down below.

4. Fire in the windlass, fire in the chain;
   It's fetch a bucket o' water girls, and put it out again.

5. Fire up aloft, and fire down below;
   It's fetch a bucket o' water girls, there's fire down below.

Shallow Brown.

(HALLIARDS.)

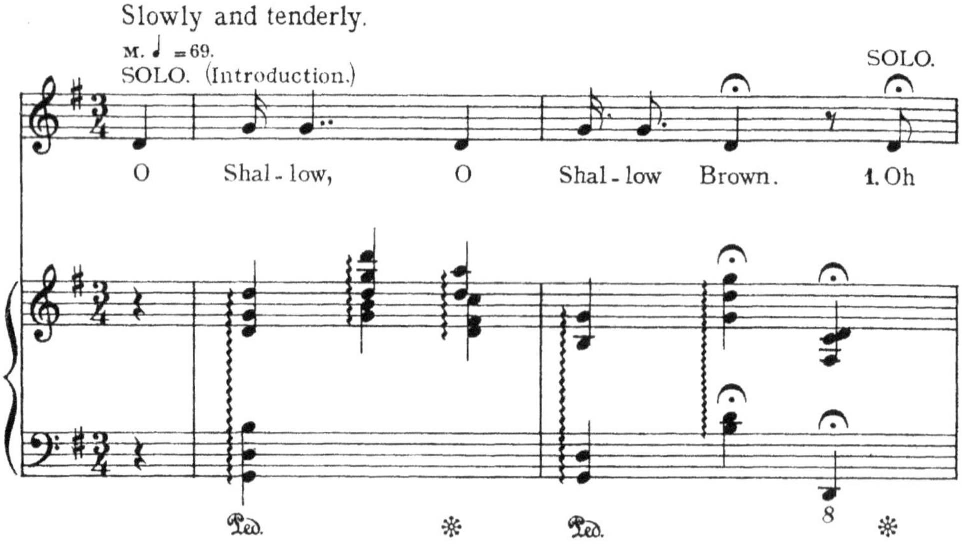

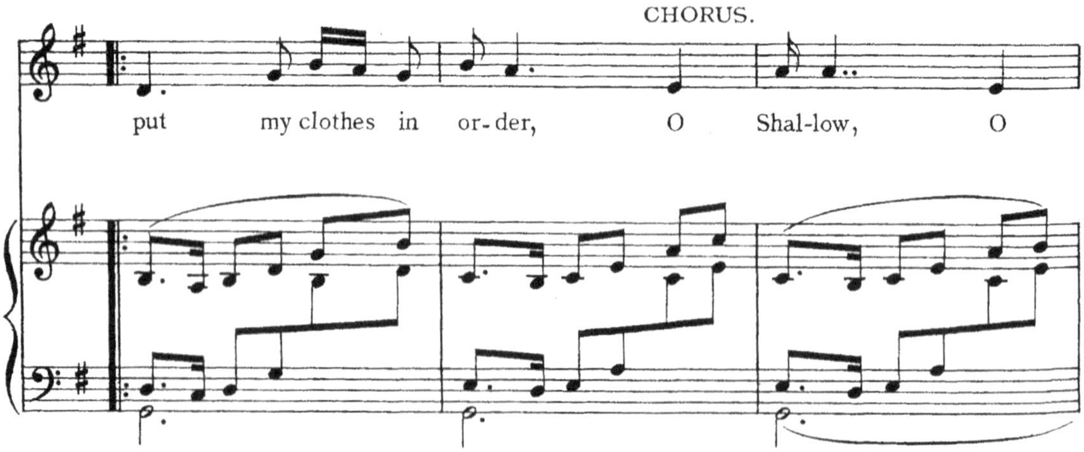

2. Away, I'm bound to leave you.
   I never will deceive you.

3. I love to look upon you.
   I bet my money on you.

4. O, Shallow in the morning,
   Just as the day was dawning.

5. Oh put my clothes in order;
   I'm bound across the border.

A long time ago.

(HALLIARDS.)

With an easy swing.

M. ♩.= 96.

SOLO.

1. A long, long time and a

CHORUS.

ve - ry long time To me way ay_____ ay ah. A

SOLO.

2. Away down South where I was born,
   Among the fields of golden corn.

3. A Yankee packet lay out in the bay,
   A-waiting a fair wind to get under weigh.

4. There once was a family lived on a hill,
   And if they're not dead they're all living there still.

Won't you go my way?

(HALLIARDS.)

2. In the morning bright and early.

3. O Juliar, Ann, Mariar.

4. I asked that girl to marry.

5. O marry, do not tarry.

6. She said she'd rather tarry.

Hilo, John Brown.

(HALLIARDS.)

2. Sally she a 'Badian bright Mulatter;
   Sally pretty gal, but can't get at her.

3. Seven long years I courted Sally;
   Sally she would flirt but nebber marry.

4. Stand to your ground and walk him up lively,
   Or de mate come around a-dingin' and a-dangin'.

Roll the cotton down.

(HALLIARDS.)

2. In the morning bright and early *(twice)*

3. So early in the morning
   Before the day was dawning.

4. We'll screw him up so cheerly *(twice)*

5. I'm off across the border   *(twice)*

6. Farewell, I'm bound to leave you;
   I never will deceive you.

Round the corner Sally.

(HALLIARDS.)

SOLO.

1. O   a _ round   the cor _ ner   we will   go.

2. To Madam Gashee's we all will go,
For Madamoiselle you all do know.

3. O Madamoiselle we'll take her in tow;
We'll take her in tow to Callao

4. O I wish I was at Madam Gashee's;
It's there we'll sit and take our ease.

The bully boat is coming.

(HALLIARDS.)

SOLO.

1. O the bul-ly boat is com-ing, Don't you hear the pad-dles

CHORUS.   SOLO.

rol-ling? Ran-do, Ran-do, hoo-ray, hoo-ray. Oh the

bul - ly boat's a - com - ing, Don't you hear the pad - dles roll - ing?

CHORUS.   VERSES 1 to 4.   SOLO.   LAST VERSE.

Ran - do,   Ran - do,   ray. _____ 2. O the   ray. _____

2. O the bully boat is coming, }
     Down the Mississippi floating. } *(twice)*

3. Oh I'm bound away to leave you, }
     And I never will deceive you. } *(twice)*

4. When I come again to meet you, }
     It's with kisses I will greet you. } *(twice)*

5. Oh the bully boat is coming,
     Don't you hear the paddles rolling? } *(twice)*

My Tommy's gone away.

(HALLIARDS.)

SOLO.

1. Tom - my's gone, what shall I do? My

CHORUS.

2. Tommy's gone to Liverpool,
   To Liverpool, that noted school.

3. Tommy's gone to Baltimore,
   Oh Tommy's gone to Baltimore.

4. Tommy's gone to Mobile Bay,
   To screw the cotton by the day.

5. Tommy's gone for evermore,
   Oh Tommy's gone for evermore.

Sing fare you well.

(HALLIARDS.)

SOLO

CHORUS.

1. Fare you well, I wish you well. Hoo - raw_____ and

2. O fare you well my bonny young gel *(twice)*

3. As I walked out one morning fair
   It's there I met a lady fair.

4. At her I winked I do declare *(twice)*

5. Up aloft this yard must go *(twice)*

6. I thought I heard the skipper say,
   One more pull and then belay.

7. Fare you well, I wish you well;
   Fare you well till I return.

*This note will be used only in Verses 3 & 4.

O Billy Riley.

(HALLIARDS.)

2. O Mister Riley, Ö Missus Riley *(twice)*

3. O Missy Riley, little Missy Riley *(twice)*

4. O Missy Riley, screw him up so cheer'ly *(twice)*

Time for us to leave her.

(HALLIARDS.)

Solo: 1. Oh times is hard and wa - ges low.

Chorus: Leave her, John - ny, leave her.

Solo: Oh

CHORUS.

times is hard and wa - ges low. 'Tis time for us to

VERSES 1 to 7.   SOLO.   LAST VERSE.

leave her. _____ (2.) Me' - leave her. _____

2. Me'og'ny beef and weevill'd bread!
   I wish old Weather-phiz was dead.

3. The rain it rains the 'ole day long;
   The Nor'–East wind is blowin' strong.

4. It's pump or drown the old man said. *(twice)*

5. I thought I heard the captain say
   "To-morrow you shall have your pay."

6. O what will us poor shellbacks do? *(twice)*

7. We'll pack up our traps and go on shore. *(twice)*

8. O times is hard and wages low. *(twice)*

Lizer Lee.

(HALLIARDS.)

2. Oh Lizer Lee she slighted me;
   Now she will not marry me.

3. When I sailed across the sea,
   Lizer said she'd be true to me.

4. I promised her a golden ring. *(twice)*

5. Up aloft this yard must go,
   Mister Mate he told us so.

6. I thought I heard the skipper say,
   "One more pull and then belay."

A hundred years on the eastern shore.

(HALLIARDS.)

2. In the Black Ball Line I served my time. *(twice)*

3. A hundred years is a very long time. *(twice)*

4. A hundred years have passed and gone. *(twice)*

5. A hundred years will come once more. *(twice)*

Walk him along, Johnny.

(HALLIARDS.)

M. ♩.=60.   SOLO.

1. Gen -'ral Tay - lor
2. Dan O' Con - nell

gained   the day.)
died long a - go.)

CHORUS.

Walk him a - long, John-ny,   car-ry him a - long.

SOLO.

Gen - 'ral Tay - lor   gained   the day.)
Dan   O' Con - nell   died long a - go.)

CHORUS.

Car-ry him to___ the

bur - y - ing ground. Then a - way - ay you Storm - y,

Walk him a - long, John-ny, car-ry him a - long. Way - ay you

Storm - y, Car - ry him to the bur - y - ing ground.

Hilonday.

(HALLIARDS.)

Bo-ney was a war-rior, Ah hi-lon-day. Oh___ rise you up, my
yel-ler gels, Ah hi-lon--day___ 2. Oh -day.

2. Oh Boney beat the Rooshans.
   Oh Boney beat the Prooshans.

3. Oh Boney went to Moscow. *(twice)*

4. Oh Moscow was afire. *(twice)*

5. Oh Boney was defeated. *(twice)*

6. Oh drive her, captain, drive her. *(twice)*

7. Oh captain, make her nŏse blood. *(twice)*

Stormalong.

(HALLIARDS.)

Slowly.

M. ♩ = 104.

SOLO.

1. Oh

Stor - my he is dead and gone. To me way you storm a -

CHORUS.

Ped. ※ Ped. ※

2. I dug his grave with a silver spade.

3. I lowered him down with a golden chain.

4. We carried him away tö Mobile Bay.

5. We'll never see his like again.

6. Stormy was ä good old man.

7. Stormy he is dead and gone.

So handy me gels.

(HALLIARDS.)

M. ♩.= 76.

SOLO.

1. So

han-dy me gels, so han - dy! Why can't you be___ so

han - dy O?   Han-dy me gels,   so han - dy!

CHORUS.

2. Be handy with your washing, girls,
   Because my love's a dandy, O.

3. My love she is a dandy, O,
   And she is fond of brandy, O.

4. O shake her up and away we'll go;
   Up aloft from down below.

The Sailor likes his bottle, O.

(INTERCHANGEABLE SHANTY.)

M. $\flat$ = 72.

1. So

INTRODUCTION.

ear - ly in the morn - ing The sail - or likes — his

SOLO.

bot - tle O. A bot - tle o' rum and a

2. So early in the morning,
   The sailor likes his baccy, O.
      A packet o' shag, and a packet o' twist,
      And a packet o' Yankee Doodle, O.
                              Chorus.

3. So early in the morning,
   The sailor likes the lasses, O.
      The lasses o' Blyth, and the lasses o' Shields,
      And the lasses across the water, O.
                              Chorus.

Haul away, Joe. II.

(FORE-SHEET OR SWEATING-UP.)

SOLO.

1. Way,   haul a - way,_____ We'll

CHORUS.

haul a - way the bow - lin'. A - way, haul a -

VERSES 1 to 4.　SOLO.　LAST VERSE.

-way,_____ Oh haul a - way, Joe. (2.) Oh Joe.

Ped.　　※

2. Oh once I had a nigger gel, and she was fat and läzy.

3. And then I had an Irish gel; she nearly druv me cräzy.

4. King Louis was the king o' France before the revolütion.

5. King Louis got his head cut off and spoiled his constitütion.

N.B. Any of the verses of "Haul away, Joe" No. I. ("The Shanty Book Part I" page 56) can be sung to this Shanty.

- 159 -

**For the Finest in
Nautical and Historical
Fiction and Nonfiction**

www.FireshipPress.com

Interesting • Informative • Authoritative

All Fireship Press books are now available
directly through www.FireshipPress.com, amazon.com
and via leading bookstores from coast-to-coast

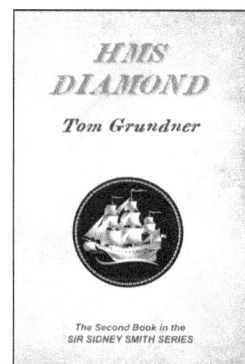

CPSIA information can be obtained
at www.ICGtesting.com
Printed in the USA
BVHW011018281221
625053BV00016B/505